THE GREAT WHEEL
WINTER

© Amy Griswold

About the Author

Jo Graham is the author of twenty-five books and two online games. Best known for her historical fantasy and her tie-in novels for MGM's popular *Stargate Atlantis* and *Stargate SG-1* series, she has been a Locus Award finalist, an Amazon Top Choice, a Spectrum Award finalist, a Romantic Times Top Pick in historical fiction, and a Lambda Literary Award and Rainbow Award nominee for bisexual fiction. With Melissa Scott, she is the author of five books in the Order of the Air series, a historical fantasy series set in the 1920s and thirties within a Hermetic Lodge.

She has practiced in Pagan and Hermetic traditions for more than thirty years, including leading an eclectic circle for nearly a decade. Dedicated in 1989, she took her mastery in 2004. She has studied the classical world extensively and today mainly works in traditions based on the Hellenistic Cult of Isis. Though she worked in politics for fifteen years, today Jo Graham divides her time between writing and working as a guardian ad litem for children in foster care. She lives in North Carolina with her partner and their daughters.

····· JO GRAHAM ·····

THE GREAT WHEEL
WINTER

RITUALS TO THRIVE
IN THE DARK CYCLE
OF THE SAECULUM

Llewellyn Publications
Woodbury, Minnesota

FIRST EDITION
First Printing, 2020

Cover design by Shannon McKuhen
Editing by Samantha Lu Sherratt
Interior art by the Llewellyn Art Department

Llewellyn Publications is a registered trademark of Llewellyn Worldwide Ltd.

Library of Congress Cataloging-in-Publication Data
Names: Graham, Jo (Jo Wyrick), author.
Title: Winter : rituals to thrive in the dark cycle of the saeculum / Jo Graham.
Description: FIRST EDITION. | Woodbury, Minnesota : Llewellyn Publications
    2020. | Includes bibliographical references.
Identifiers: LCCN 2020000797 (print) | LCCN 2020000798 (ebook) | ISBN
    9780738763712 (paperback) | ISBN 9780738764115 (ebook)
Subjects: LCSH: Rites and ceremonies. | Winter—Miscellanea.
Classification: LCC BL595.W55 G73 2020 (print) | LCC BL595.W55 (ebook) |
    DDC 299/.94—dc23
LC record available at https://lccn.loc.gov/2020000797
LC ebook record available at https://lccn.loc.gov/2020000798

Llewellyn Worldwide Ltd. does not participate in, endorse, or have any authority or responsibility concerning private business transactions between our authors and the public.

All mail addressed to the author is forwarded but the publisher cannot, unless specifically instructed by the author, give out an address or phone number.

Any internet references contained in this work are current at publication time, but the publisher cannot guarantee that a specific location will continue to be maintained. Please refer to the publisher's website for links to authors' websites and other sources.

Llewellyn Publications
A Division of Llewellyn Worldwide Ltd.
2143 Wooddale Drive
Woodbury, MN 55125-2989
www.llewellyn.com
Printed in the United States of America

Other Books by Jo Graham

The Great Wheel

for my granny, Elma, who stood here before me

Contents

Introduction: Charting Our Course

····· **Chapter 1** ·····

A Sailor on the Seas of Time

The morning of September 11, 2001, I was supposed to go to Washington, DC. I had planned to fly out of Raleigh-Durham Airport, a smaller regional airport with little security, but my partner was squirrely about it. She had a bad feeling, she said, and that was so rare for her that I agreed to take the train instead. At 8:30 a.m. I was in my office checking my email, my luggage beside my desk, ready to take a cab to the train station in an hour and a half.

You know what happened next. Breaking news bulletins, the phone ringing off the hook, everyone under the sun calling and comparing notes. My coworker came in. He was trying to get information, but there wasn't much. A plane had hit the World Trade Center. Maybe it was two planes. What in the world was happening?

I called my friend Liz in DC, the one with whom I was supposed to be staying that night. Should I still come? What was up? Liz and I were talking and then suddenly she said, "Oh God."

"What?" I said.

"Something's wrong," she said. "I heard a boom and out my window I can see a plume of smoke rising from down toward the mall." And through the phone I heard it: every siren in DC blasting, every emergency vehicle tearing down the street outside her window, the old civil defense sirens shouting out their warnings of nuclear war or air raid. A plane had hit the Pentagon.

We stayed on the phone another few minutes. "I have to go," Liz said. "A police officer just came in and said we all have to go to the air-raid shelter in the basement. Bye."

My coworker had found a TV. We watched Tom Brokaw. My partner called. "Are you still going to DC?"

"If the train is running, I'm going," I said. "It's politics. It's important."

She swore up and down, but she didn't try to talk me out of it. But they halted the trains. They grounded the planes.

My coworker and I watched the towers fall. I worried about Karen, a friend who worked a few blocks away.

At last, we had to stop. He took the TV back into his office. The phone stopped ringing. "I'm going down to the sandwich shop," he said. "Do you want anything?" It was one o'clock.

"Sure," I said. I didn't know how it had gotten so late. I went in my office and closed the door. I stood in the corner window of this old office building, looking out toward the airport at something that I had never seen in my lifetime—a planeless sky. It stretched blue and perfect, not a single contrail, not a single flash of silver on approach to Raleigh-Durham. From the seventh floor I could always see planes.

And so I looked down, not at the bright sky but at the other buildings. There was the Department of Revenue building, its art deco façade proclaiming it had been built in the thirties. My granny had worked there, one of many women bookkeepers. Had she stood at that window on the morning of December 8, 1941, that cold Monday after Pearl Harbor? I could almost see her there. I could see her standing in the window, her hair in braids across the top of her head, a black dress because it was winter, her hands on the sill as she looked out across two blocks and sixty years. Could she see me? Could she imagine the daughter of her son, who was then a college freshman, looking back? No; she was thinking of him. She was thinking of her freshman son and war. She could not imagine me here saying, "Granny, it's ok. He won't be fine but he'll come through it and there will be two granddaughters and right now you're widowed only a year and your heart is in pieces, but you will love again and he'll be a really super guy, and I promise your son will live.

You will do things in the next ten years you can't imagine, and you'll do your best to save the world, and someday I will be looking back at you, two blocks and sixty years away."

I could almost feel her presence, not as she was then but as I last knew her, as if she were saying, "I don't know what this crisis holds for you. But I do know this: you're strong. You'll get through winter. We always do."

And so we do. The wheel turns and turns again. Winter follows autumn and spring follows winter. We are not lost in a trackless sea. We are following the paths of wind and wave that those before us have navigated.

I am a novelist, and before that I spent more than a decade as a political operative. I am a historian by training. If you want to understand what the tides will do, ask a sailor. The way to understand the tides is to know the sea, to understand her patterns and her currents, the pull of the moon and the way of the waves. Knowing these patterns shows the sailor what course to set. It allows the sailor to predict what conditions will be based on what conditions have been in the past—not just the immediate past but the long past of experience. The way to understand what will happen in the future is to understand history and the patterns that govern it. I am a sailor on the seas of time. So are you. This book is a navigational chart to this sea of Winter, an atlas to our present season.

First, we will examine the great patterns, the currents that flow beneath the surface and underlie history as we live it: the Great Wheel of the Saeculum. We will examine the patterns, regular as the tides in their waxing and waning and as natural. They are part of the world. Just as the Wheel of the Year turns round and round, so the Great Wheel turns across human life spans. We will review the seasons of the saeculum, which have been discussed in more detail in my book *The Great Wheel*.

Then we will examine more closely the last time we voyaged here, our last saecular Winter from 1925–1945. While very few of us have traveled those waters ourselves because it was eighty years ago, we have many charts created by those who were here before us. We'll examine these precious stories, consider what we can learn from them, and ask those who have gone before us to help us navigate this current crisis.

Next we will look at the beginnings of our current Winter. We will consider who we were and where we stood when Autumn changed to Winter. In order to understand where to go, both as individuals and as a society, we need to understand how we got here. Through journaling and meditation, we will explore our story in the context of the cycle so far.

Then we will take an in-depth look at the phases of Winter, examining each of them in turn—what we can expect and what steps we need to take to survive and thrive in this era of crisis. We can't make Winter go away or make the season change faster than it naturally will, but we can take steps to safeguard ourselves, our loved ones, and our communities as this storm deepens. In other words, our knowledge of the sea tells us as sailors that a storm is upon us. Our skill as sailors can see us through. Through stories, exercises, and rituals, we will chart our course through this crisis.

Lastly, we will look forward at what happens next. Before 2030, Spring will come. What will that be like? Looking at the patterns and at current trends, we will examine the transition to Spring and discuss the "long-range forecast" for the coming season.

I invite you to join me on this voyage. Together, let us put forth bravely.

····· **Chapter 2** ·····

Seasons of the Saeculum

Time is cyclical, a series of interlocking circles that follow the same pattern year after year, century after century. The moon waxes and wanes every month as it goes through its phases—first quarter, full, last quarter, new—predictably and regularly. The Wheel of the Year turns. While the cycle manifests itself differently in different climates, it follows the same pattern year after year. For example, in ancient Egypt there was the season of the inundation, followed by planting and growth, followed by harvest, followed by the dry season waiting for the flood again.[1] In temperate climates we experience spring and planting, summer and growth, autumn and harvest, winter and cold. The wheel turns on and on, year after year, century after century.

There is also a larger wheel, the wheel of human life, which is composed of four phases of life. The Romans called these *pueritia* (childhood), *iuventus* (youth), *virilitas* (maturity), and *senectia* (old age). According to Roman writers, these phases correspond with the seasons. We are children in springtime, are filled with the passions of youth in summer, grow to maturity in autumn, and grow old with the year in winter. The wheel of our lives turns just as the Wheel of the Year does, and unless we die young and untimely, we will experience all four seasons.

---

1. deTraci Regula, *The Mysteries of Isis* (St. Paul, MN: Llewellyn Publications, 1996).

However, there is an even larger wheel that the Romans called "the Great Wheel," or the *saeculum*, the wheel of generations, and its cycle is about eighty years long. Society has seasons too. There is a new beginning in the aftermath of a crisis in Spring, the growth of new institutions and ideas in Summer, overreach and conflict in Autumn, and a new crisis coming to a head in Winter. This is a pattern we see over and over again. If we live a long life, eighty years or more, we will live through each season and return to the season of our birth.

Each generation is born in a particular season, and that shapes how they experience the Great Wheel. For example, a person who is born in Spring enters the world when the crises have been resolved, when people are optimistic about the future, and when life seems safe and stable for most people. Their young adulthood is in Summer, when exciting new ideas can be explored and freedom is the greatest good. The last two Spring-born generations, the Baby Boomers and the Missionary Generation born in the late Victorian period, had this experience.

However, someone who is born in Autumn has a very different experience. They are born when shadows are lengthening, when the world is seeming an increasingly fragmented, combative, and unsafe place. The Crisis era, Winter, hits them in young adulthood, calling on them to be the heroes and rebuilders. The last two Autumn-born generations, the Greatest Generation and the Millennials, had this experience.[2]

In other words, each person who lives a long life sees all four seasons but at different points in their life, which makes their lived experience extremely different. This chart illustrates this:

Generation	Youth	Adulthood	Maturity	Old Age
Spring-born	Spring	Summer	Autumn	Winter
Summer-born	Summer	Autumn	Winter	Spring
Autumn-born	Autumn	Winter	Spring	Summer
Winter-born	Winter	Spring	Summer	Autumn

2. William Strauss and Neil Howe, *Generations* (New York: Morrow and Company, 1991).

So who are you? The oldest generation living today is the Greatest Generation, born from 1905 to 1925. This is the generation that fought World War II and built the new, shining Tomorrowland America of the 1950s. They were Autumn-born in the last saeculum. In 2020, the youngest of them are 95 years old.

The next generation, and the first still highly influential in public life in 2020, is the Silent Generation, born from 1926 to 1942. Too young for World War II and too old to be hippies, this is the generation of Nancy Pelosi, Ruth Bader Ginsburg, and Bernie Sanders. The youngest of this generation are 78 in 2020, and their influence is waning. They are the Winter-born generation born during the last crises, the Great Depression and World War II.

They are followed by the Baby Boomers, born 1943–1960. In 2020 this is the generation that holds the most power, including Donald Trump, Elizabeth Warren, and Chief Justice John Roberts. Spring-born, they came of age in the 1960s and 1970s.

Next comes Generation X, born 1961–1980. Their influence is rising as they enter their most powerful years. Summer-born, they came of age in the darkening years of the 1980s and 1990s. In 2020 the oldest are 59 and the youngest 40.

After them come the Millennials, born 1981 to perhaps 2001. (The dividing line between Millennials and Homelanders isn't clear yet.) In 2020 they will all have come of age, with the youngest about 19 and the oldest 39, passing the Baby Boomers as the largest voting bloc. Autumn-born, they have always known a darkening world.

Last are the Homelanders, born 2002 or since. They are born in the Winter of this current crisis and are children and teenagers in 2020.

As we reach the climax of this current Crisis era, each generation has a unique role to play. The Silent are the elder statesmen and the seasoned community leaders. The Baby Boomers precipitate the crisis and have leadership roles on all sides. They set the parameters of the conflict. Generation X provides the practical, on-the-ground, day-to-day expertise. They end the conflict. The Millennials fight the conflict. They are the young participants. The Homelanders are mostly too young to be part of the conflict, but they are shaped by it for their dominant role as the wheel turns, in their season of Summer.

The Seasons of the Great Wheel

The Great Wheel, like the Wheel of the Year, is divided into octaves. These are approximately ten years long, the full circle of the wheel being approximately eighty years—the length of a human life. We are all familiar with the basic diagram of the Wheel of the Year as it's commonly presented in Paganism today:

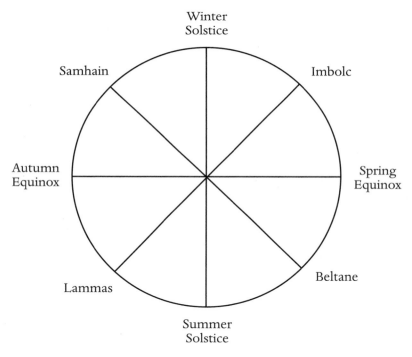

We travel around the wheel clockwise, experiencing each season in its turn. There is no way to skip a season or to turn the wheel backward and return to a previous season without going all the way around the wheel.

The Great Wheel applies this concept to the Great Wheel of the Saeculum. In Spring, society has big plans and is optimistic and sees enormous growth. In Summer some of those plans come to fruition and others become sources of conflict as ideologies emerge that would lead society in different directions. The apparent consensus of Spring is broken. In Autumn growth slows, creating a dimmer mood as the conflicts become more apparent. In Winter those conflicts erupt into a crisis, often into actual war by the end of the era. There are winners and losers. Conflicts are resolved, conclusions are reached, and the cycle begins again.

If we mapped the seasons of the great year, the diagram of the last eighty years would look like this:

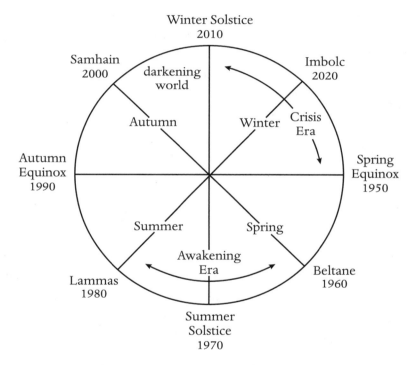

In 1950 we stood at Spring Equinox. World War II was over, the economy was booming, and we stood at the beginning of a long optimistic period in American history, when it seemed like science and law could make tomorrow better than today. Bigger, brighter, faster—there was nothing we couldn't do!

1960 brought us President Kennedy's promise to put a man on the moon by the end of the decade, and the sixties were a wild ride from the pastel-Chanel-suit-and-pillbox-hat beginnings to Woodstock and the Vietnam War —the season of Beltane in all its fire.

By 1970 Summer was upon us in earnest, hot and ripe with conflicts that erupted to disrupt the American high and slowly, ever so slowly, begin our turn to the dark of the year. The summer's longest day is at midsummer. After that we were already descending, though it may not have been apparent.

1980 was our Lammas, the first harvest and a ripe, rich time. Conflicts brewed beneath the surface, but our national institutions seemed strong and our power infallible.

Fall Equinox came in 1990 with riches being reaped by many and those who were left behind being easy to ignore because Yuppies and Babies on Board dominated the national consciousness.

2000 brought us Samhain, a turn to the dark. Seasons don't always arrive precisely on the date, but Samhain truly began on September 11, 2001. Our national season of Winter had begun.

2010 was our Winter Solstice, when it became clear that we were in the midst of Winter and that storms would surely overtake us soon. Conflicts of all kinds dominated the national discourse.

In 2020 we stand at Imbolc with the worst of this Winter's storms ahead and Spring still distant beyond the horizon. This is where we are.

Ekpyrosis and Rebirth

Just as each year in the Wheel of the Year experiences winter, so does each cycle of the great year experience saecular Winter. This is, quite simply, a time of crisis. Every eighty years we pass through what the Classical Greeks called *ekpyrosis*, a destruction by fire that then allows for rebirth and the growth of new things. This is not like the Christian concept of apocalypse, which is about disasters that signify the end of the world. Ekpyrosis is the mechanism by which the world ends and begins anew.

Imagine a volcanic eruption like the eruption of Mount St. Helens in the state of Washington in 1980. Thousands of tons of superheated ash and rock were released, blowing debris into the stratosphere. The shockwave leveled forests. The cloud of ash overwhelmed everyone in its way, including scientists taking pictures of the event, their cameras recovered later to show that they kept filming even as they were overtaken. Nearly sixty people were killed. Fifteen hundred elk and five thousand deer died, as well as twelve million fish and countless smaller animals. The crater left behind was two miles wide, and ash fell from Seattle to Spokane. Photos taken afterward show a complete wasteland, a desert of ash marked with the skeletons of burned trees. It seemed impossible that the beautiful forest could ever return.[3]

Arriving just a few days after the eruption, ecologist Charlie Crisafulli saw nothing but destruction. He said, "It looked like everything had been destroyed, that all vestiges of life had been snuffed out."[4] And yet as he investigated, he saw that the high lakes had been protected by ice, their plants and animals still alive beneath the surface. Ants scurried through the ash. Moss survived and spread over downed trees. A gopher emerged from its burrow, having literally ridden out the eruption in its underground bunker.

Within a year, wildflowers bloomed, forests transformed into meadows, birds came to eat the seeds, and pollinators thrived. Alder and willow seedlings began to grow where huge fir trees once had.

Twenty years later, young hardwood trees began to make groves, attracting elk and deer. The streams and lakes once again teemed with fish. Chipmunks, squirrels, and songbirds were plentiful.[5]

Now, nearly forty years later, the big trees are coming back. There's a forest again, albeit not yet an old-growth forest, but it has understory plants like lily of the valley and animals like foxes drawn by the plentiful wildlife. Once again the elk thrive. The giant fir trees are saplings coming up through the understory.

This is ekpyrosis. There is disaster and then recovery. The new thing isn't exactly like the old thing, but new things grow surprisingly quickly. The world ends and then begins. This is as true of societies as it is of forest ecosystems. Just as the natural geologic cycle drives the eruption of volcanoes, the cycle of the saeculum drives the rebirth of human societies.

---

3. Robert I. Tilling, Lyn Topinka, and Donald A. Swanson, "Eruptions of Mount Saint Helens: Past, Present, and Future," United States Geological Survey, 2002, https://pubs.er.usgs.gov/publication/7000010.

4. Charlie Crisafulli, "35 Years after Mount St. Helens Eruption, Nature Returns," interview by Michael Casey, CBS News, May 18, 2015, https://www.cbsnews.com/news/35-years-after-mt-st-helens-eruption-nature-returns/.

5. Michael Casey, "35 Years after Mount St. Helens Eruption, Nature Returns," CBS News, May 18, 2015, https://www.cbsnews.com/news/35-years-after-mt-st-helens-eruption-nature-returns/.

Date	Octave	National Mood	Elders (Senectia)	Maturity (Virilitas)	Youth (Iuventus)	Childhood (Pueritia)
1900	Lammas	complex and challenged	Gilded	Progressive and Missionary	Missionary	Lost
1910	Autumn Equinox	fracturing	Gilded and Progressive	Progressive and Missionary	Missionary and Lost	Lost and Greatest
1920	Samhain	darkening	Progressive	Missionary	Lost	Greatest
1930	Winter Solstice	moving toward crisis	Progressive and Missionary	Missionary and Lost	Lost and Greatest	Greatest and Silent
1940	Imbolc	grim	Missionary	Lost	Greatest	Silent
1950	Spring Equinox	resurgent and hopeful	Missionary and Lost	Lost and Greatest	Greatest and Silent	Silent and Baby Boom
1960	Beltane	conformist and optimistic	Missionary and Lost	Greatest	Silent	Baby Boom
1970	Summer Solstice	frenetic and free	Lost and Greatest	Greatest and Silent	Silent and Baby Boom	Baby Boom and Generation X
1980	Lammas	complex and challenged	Lost and Greatest	Silent	Baby Boom	Generation X

Date	Octave	National Mood	Elders (Senectia)	Maturity (Virilitas)	Youth (Iuventus)	Childhood (Pueritia)
1990	Autumn Equinox	fracturing	Greatest and Silent	Silent and Baby Boom	Baby Boom and Generation X	Generation X and Millennials
2000	Samhain	divided and darkening	Greatest and Silent	Baby Boom	Generation X	Millennials
2010	Winter Solstice	moving toward crisis	Silent and Baby Boom	Baby Boom and Generation X	Generation X and Millennials	Millennials and Homelanders
2020	Imbolc	grim	Silent and Baby Boom	Generation X	Millennials	Homelanders

This is the map of our past and our present. In order to understand how we move forward from here, we need to look back at previous great years. If you want to know what February is like, the best way to know is to examine your experience of previous Februaries. The best way to understand what happens next in the great year is to examine our experience of previous saecula. However, because the cycle of the great year is eighty years long, most of us have not experienced the season we are in before.

However, others have. Other generations that share the same birth position on the Great Wheel as us have stood in the same season. Their experiences can guide us, just as a mariner on unfamiliar seas is guided by the charts and notes of those who sailed this way before. Let's take a quick look back at how the previous saecula have worked and how each generation's role has developed. (A much more thorough and complex treatment of each octave of the Great Wheel can be found in my book, *The Great Wheel*, in which I go deeply into each season of the great year and how it is experienced and expressed by each generation.)

The scholars William Strauss and Neil Howe exhaustively examined these cycles in American history in their book, *Generations*, which I encourage you to read if you are interested in an in-depth look at the historical cycles. However, to sum up their work briefly, we can see this cycle at work if we simply look at the dates.

In 1945 World War II ended, the end of a Crisis era that had convulsed the world. Eighty years earlier, in 1865, the Civil War ended, concluding another Crisis era. Eighty-two years earlier, the Treaty of Paris of 1783 ended the American Revolution. Strauss and Howe continue back more or less in eighty-year increments. In 1692 the Salem Witch Trials ended a Crisis era that determined whether the American colonies would be a Puritan state or not. In 1588 the Armada Crisis concluded England's wars with Spain, determining whether the dominant power and culture in North America would be English or Spanish.[6] Since the early modern era, these cycles of ekpyrosis and rebirth have been apparent in American life.

---

6. Strauss and Howe, *Generations*.

Now it's time for that part of the cycle again. Count eighty years forward from 1945 and you reach 2025. The upheavals we are experiencing are not unnatural or unprecedented. They are a natural part of the cycle of history, of the Great Wheel.

This makes the times we live in no less dangerous! The Spanish Armada, the Salem Witch Trials, the Civil War, World War II—all were critical, dangerous moments that changed the lives of millions. We are deep in Winter, about to pass through the fire of ekpyrosis, with the time of new growth and rebirth still some years away. How do we live in these times?

This book seeks to answer that question, first by examining how our ancestors did it, then by providing positive steps that we can take now and in the next few years, and lastly by helping us create the institutions and circumstances that will allow us to weather the storms and find our way safely to port.

····· Chapter 3 ·····

Last Winter

1928

It is a cool night in early autumn, and a group of six people have gathered around the dining table in a neat little bungalow on a quiet street. To anyone driving past, the muted lights behind drawn living room curtains and the three cars parked in the driveway and on the street would make it appear that the young couple who live here are having a small party—perhaps dinner or a card party—but what is actually happening is a far more mysterious gathering. The round dining table is spread with an elaborate embroidered cloth: a sixteen-pointed star in bright reds and yellows worked on blue and encircled to create a mandala; gold fringe, two inches long, drips on all sides. There's a candelabra in the center of the table, the only light in the dining room. A young woman in her late twenties is suggesting where her guests should sit—her friend to her left, her husband's friend on the other side, then the other married couple present, and then her husband at her right, where he will be the ground to her spark in the energy that goes around the table. She's a Leo, born under the bright summer sun in August of 1900, while he's a clever, trickster Scorpio, born in the fall of 1895. It's important that the table be seated correctly to balance the elemental energies of the participants. She has bobbed brown hair, greenish-hazel eyes, and a gamine smile to go with her forceful personality.

On the table in front of her is a small silver box, the kind that ladies keep on their dressing tables, and it contains a slender gold chain. As her guests settle into their chairs, she takes a deep breath and loops the chain through her wedding band so that the ring hangs freely. She puts her right elbow on the table, the chain holding the ring suspended from the middle finger of her right hand. She experimentally allows the chain to swing free.

"That's just your wedding ring," her friend says. Perhaps she had expected something more occult. She's never been to one of these before.

"It's something I have a close connection to," the woman says. "That's the most important thing. I wear it all the time. It's psychically tuned to me."

"Like my sword," her husband says, glancing at a US Army dress saber resting on the sideboard. "It's part of the uniform, but it comes from my commissioning, and I use it in Lodge."

There's a tug at the back of her dress, and the woman twists around in her chair. A little blond boy about 4 years old is standing there. "Mama, can I stay for the séance?"

His father scoops him up. "Not tonight, Bunky. You're too young."

"But I want to see the ghosts!"

"We're not talking to any ghosts tonight," his mother says. "Now let Daddy take you back to bed. It's nearly nine o'clock." As father and son disappear into the small second bedroom, she takes a deep breath. "Let's close our eyes and join hands so that we can balance our energies before we begin."

———— • ————

Today, there is the popular misconception that New Age spiritual traditions are either folklore handed down in isolated ethnic enclaves or were invented in the 1960s and 1970s. Meanwhile, Pagans point to resurgences and rediscoveries of ancient traditions from the medieval or ancient world. Both views tend to forget that there has been a vibrant Western magical tradition in the United States all along, and that just as awareness of various spiritual paths expanded in the 1990s and 2000s, so it did before, in the last Autumn and Winter in the 1920s and 1930s.

The Lost Generation embraced concepts from the Spiritualist Movement like séances and popularized tarot cards and pendulum dowsing. Ouija boards, which had been invented in 1890, became a serious, if already contro-versial, tool for conversing with the spirit world.[7] Likewise, the Rider-Waite tarot deck, published in 1910 with glorious illustrations by Pamela Colman Smith, simplified and made divination with cards more accessible.[8] Other strands, like interest in psychic research, emerged as a way of examining ghosts, precognition, and other phenomena through the lens of science. The Rhine Institute, founded in 1930, is one of the oldest parapsychological re-search centers in the world and brought these ideas to a larger audience.[9] Just as it happens today, individuals and small groups melded new tools and ideas with earlier strands of belief and with the teachings of formal organizations and Lodges that had sprung up in the late nineteenth century.

This ritual is an example of this. The young woman using her wedding ring to pendulum dowse claims a Scottish grandmother with the Sight, while she herself is using the trappings of the Spiritualist Movement—the candles, tablecloth, and pendulum. She also practices bibliomancy, which is saying a certain traditional prayer and opening the Bible at random. The verse that is immediately apparent is the advice offered. This is a very old form of divi-nation that was attested to in the seventeenth century in the writings of Ra-belais. It must have been newly widespread then, since it depends on literacy and owning a copy of the Bible, things that would not have been common in an earlier era.

Meanwhile, her husband has brought the trappings of a more formal Lodge tradition, possibly from his membership in a Masonic or quasi-Masonic Lodge, including the energy work and the use of his sword as a ritual implement. He will also, in a few years, be an early respondent and research subject at the Rhine Institute. Like today's eclectic working groups, they are bringing together diverse traditions to create a unique form of American magic, one that will become "Fam-Trad."

---

7. Mitch Horowitz, *Occult America* (New York: Bantam Books, 2009), 66–68.

8. Robert M. Place, *The Tarot* (New York: Penguin, 2005).

9. "Who We Are," Rhine.org, accessed April 30, 2019, https://bit.ly/2PtGWL7.

1988

The basement is hot and stuffy, the air-conditioning just beginning to cool the house down after it has been sitting unoccupied for a few weeks. The funeral is over. The flowers have wilted, the last of the food brought to the family has been eaten. A young woman of 20 is poking through boxes, her hair in a high ponytail. She wears shorts and a tank top in the heat, her hands already dusty. A small sterling silver ankh on a chain hangs around her neck. "This box looks like men's shirts," she says, opening it a little further. That's what it is, alright—white shirts, blue shirts, plaid shirts, and a pair of polyester pants.

"We can donate those," a man says. He's in his 60s with steel-gray hair and glasses, sweating in khaki pants and a polo shirt. He's sorting hardback books into two stacks: keep and donate.

"Yeah." The girl digs a little deeper. Something bright has caught her eye, and she grabs a corner and pulls it out.

It's a tablecloth. She spreads it out on the boxes—bright reds and yellows make a sixteen-pointed star within a circle, gold fringe all around the edges, as brilliant and beautiful as when it was made. "Wow," she says. It feels amazing, like it almost crackles under her hands. "Where'd this come from, Daddy?"

He looks over and a smile spreads across his face. "I haven't seen that in a long time. That's the tablecloth my parents used for séances when I was a little kid. I didn't know she still had that."

"They had séances?"

"Lots of people had séances then. Where do you think I learned the pendulum, like I taught you?" He pulls a jeweler's loupe out of his pocket, a metal one that hangs on a long piece of string. A geologist has every reason to examine rocks, and if he should walk through a field casually swinging it, it's just fidgeting.

She runs her hands over the cloth almost reverently. "It's gorgeous."

"You can have it," he says. "I expect she'd like that."

Her eyes rove over it. "I'm going to hang it on the wall over my bed." She uses cards rather than the pendulum and her group is more Scott Cunningham than Spiritualist, but she's the only one who actually learned things from a parent rather than in the New Age section of Borders. This is beautiful, a tangible link to those who came before, and it will be treasured all through this present Autumn and into the Winter to come.

Telling Stories: An Exercise

For this you will need a way to journal or write, whether that's a blank book to write in, a word processing program on a computer, or some other means that you prefer. You are going to become a recorder of folklore—the lore of your folk, the story of your people however you define them.

Last Winter three generations were to the fore: the Missionary Generation (born 1865–1883), the Lost Generation (born 1884–1904), and the Greatest Generation (born 1905–1925). Generations are made up of individuals, and individuals have stories to tell. In this chapter we're going to look at those stories and use them to understand the season of Winter better. To understand the experience of Winter, we have to look at it through the lens of characters. That's why from early tales like the *Epic of Gilgamesh*, the *Mahabharata*, or the *Odyssey* all the way to the present, the listener is invited to experience momentous events through the eyes of those who were there. This almost goes without saying. Which is more attractive: reading a dry document or reading an adventure with a clear protagonist? In order for us to engage with history, we need to make it about someone. It needs to be someone's story.

We'll begin by simply telling a recollection, a story that we remember about someone we knew.

My Great-Aunt Maude was the only person I knew from the Missionary generation. She lived in a little brick bungalow, and I remember visiting when I was very small. I was so small that the only thing I really remember about it was that she served ice cream in green Depression glass parfait glasses. I had strawberry ice cream with whipped cream and a maraschino cherry on top and I thought it was so elegant and princess-like! I remember trying to sit up very straight in a dining chair, not a high chair, to eat it, and that my feet didn't touch the floor.

She was tall and rawboned and fragile, a little over ninety at the time, and I was told to be very careful climbing onto her lap. She smelled like rose cologne and she had a big locket around her neck. "What's in it?" I asked, and she opened it for me. There was a picture of a very handsome young man. "Who's that?" I wanted to know.

"That's your uncle Irvin," she said. "He died before you were old enough to remember."

I thought about it for a long minute and asked as tactfully as I knew how to. "So why did such a handsome young man marry an old lady like you?"

She laughed so hard that we both shook, then wiped the tears out of her eyes. "Darling, I wasn't an old lady in 1906!"

Now it's your turn. Tell a story about the oldest person you have ever known. Maybe it's a relative. Maybe it's a family friend or a mentor. Maybe it's someone you knew professionally and admired—the key thing is that this is a story that you remember. This is about someone you met, the oldest person you knew personally. It doesn't have to be profound or important. It can be, like the vignette above, just a recollection. It may be from your own early childhood, or it might be later.

Who were they? How did you know them? How old were they at the time? How old were you? In the example above, I know that she died in 1975, and I know that I was so young that I usually sat in a high chair at the table, so this memory must date to the early 1970s.

In your memory, what was the overall feeling? What kind of person do you think they were? What can you tell about them from even the limited amount of a memory? In my example, I know that she had a good sense of humor and that she liked children. Remembering it, I feel warm and happy, so I must have felt warm and happy at the time.

Now think about the setting and what it tells you about the person and the time. Think about the period details as though you were a set designer trying to make a period movie look right. Try to zero in on one or two details. In my example above, the Depression glass parfait glasses are really distinctive. Depression glass was a kind of stamped machine-made glassware that was often given away as a freebie with purchase or collected with points off various consumer goods during the Great Depression. While today it's collectible and celebrated as an American antique, with pieces that cost hundreds of dollars, at the time it was cheap—the dollar-store glassware of the day.[10] She had a complete set of green parfait glasses, no doubt collected one at a time as premiums in hard times, and she'd kept them for forty years and brought them out for entertaining. They weren't expensive in the early 1970s, so she liked them and was proud of them, and yet was willing to let a toddler great-niece eat out of them. Find a detail in your story that is telling and think about what it means. You may need to do a little research to know more about it, as I did about Depression glass.

Record your story. You have made a piece of folklore, the lore of your people, just like the bards of old.

What does this tell us about the season of Winter? See if you can find something in your story that relates to the years 1925–1945. The Depression glass example tells a great deal about life in the 1930s and about how even in very hard times people tried to make their homes welcoming and comfortable. If the people in your story lived through those years, what were they doing? Where did they live? What were their homes and their jobs like? You may not know. You may need to do some research or think about things and put them together or ask an older person who also knew them.

For example, I can't actually remember if Great-Aunt Maude worked or not, or, if she did, what her job was. She was so old when I knew her that whatever it had been was long in the past. I think Uncle Irvin sold insurance. I think I remember my father saying he bought his first insurance policy from him. They lived in a small town, the town Maude grew up in, and the house I remember dated from the twenties or thirties. Did they buy it then or later?

10. "National Depression Glass Association," Ndga.net, retrieved April 20, 2019, http://ndga.net/.

I don't know. They didn't have children, but they had a host of nieces and nephews.

Think about what you may know about the person from other sources if there are many blanks in your story. In my example, I know from my father and his cousin that Great-Aunt Maude was a strict teetotaler who believed that any consumption of alcohol was evil and that she was continually tweaked by her younger and wilder Lost Generation sisters for her righteousness. At any family event where there was beer or wine, she could be counted on to lecture whoever drank, which resulted in her Greatest Generation nephews and nieces drinking beer out in the driveway to avoid the lecture, even at Christmas when it was cold! They'd go "look at something about the car," to her apparent bafflement as to why the young people always spent so much time looking at cars, and she never did catch on that they were actually drinking beer out of a case in somebody's trunk.

A story like this leads us to one of the central conflicts between the Missionary Generation and the Lost Generation—the battle over Prohibition. The idea of abstinence from alcoholic beverages was not new. As early as 1846 organizations like the New Jersey Daughters of Temperance existed with the mission of ending alcohol consumption, with bylaws stating "no sister shall make, buy, sell or use … any spiritous or malt liquor, wine or cider, and shall always discountenance the use of them in the community."[11] However, in the Awakening period around the turn of the century, these organizations exploded into national influence, with temperance becoming one of the major culture war issues of the period. Young women of Maude's age were implored to take the pledge "lips that touch wine shall never touch mine," meaning that they would never consider courting a man who did not abstain completely from alcohol.[12] Like the purity pledges of today, the idea

---

11. "Constitution and By-Laws of the Martha Washington Salem Union No. 4 Daughters of Temperance," New Jersey Women's History, retrieved April 20, 2019, http://njwomens history.org/Period_3/daughters.htm.

12. Phineas Garrett, ed., *The Speaker's Garland* (Philadelphia, PA: The Penn Publishing Company, 1905).

was that this was something a young woman did out of a desire to be good and also to be safe.

One of the contexts of temperance as a women-led movement was that suffrage, the idea that women should have the right to vote, and temperance went hand in hand. The core idea was that women are naturally more virtuous than men, naturally more peaceful, kind, and cooperative, and that alcohol only exaggerates men's bestial qualities, leading to drunkenness, assaults, sexual misconduct, and even a newly identified crime that was not prosecutable: marital rape. If women could vote, they would immediately rid the nation of venality as their superior instincts would cause an end to war and poverty. If men were denied alcohol, they would cease to commit so many crimes, especially those against women. Therefore, women must use their civilizing influence to rein in men and their savage instincts.

There was also a strong anti-Catholic and anti-immigrant bent to the movement, which held that Protestant women, both white and African American,[13] must work to Americanize poor and ignorant Southern and Eastern European immigrants who drank as part of their culture, used wine in their religious rituals, and were violent and uncivilized. Through settlement homes and aid societies, they attempted to link assimilation to temperance. As the president of the Minnesota Women's Christian Temperance Movement said in her 1900 address, "We must have a regiment of American workers who … will work among the German children and young people until we get them to love clear brains better than beer … others must learn French and Italian and various dialects that the truths of personal purity and total abstinence may be taught to those who live among us."[14] The Women's Christian Temperance Union also espoused the idea that social pathologies, like violence and sexual misconduct, were the result of heredity and that certain peoples were more prone to them than others. The answer to this was

---

13. Glen R. Hanson, Peter J. Venturelli, and Annette E. Fleckenstein, *Drugs and Society* (New York: Jones and Bartlett, 2017), 252.

14. Kathleen Kerr, "How Did the Reform Agenda of the Minnesota Woman's Christian Temperance Union Change, 1878–1917?" (Binghamton, NY: State University of New York at Binghamton, 1998).

the availability of birth control, which would act as a positive form of eugenics to lower the birthrate of peoples with undesirable genes. If women in these populations had fewer children, and those children assimilated to Protestant American values, gradually humanity would be improved.[15]

At this point one's head may be spinning! Wait—temperance, women's rights, eugenics, access to birth control, and anti-immigrant attitudes are on the same side? On the other side is brewers and the alcohol industry, people who oppose suffrage, people who welcome immigrants, people who believe that character is formed by experience rather than genetics, and people who don't believe in evolution? What in the world?

The past is a different country. Our saeculum's constellation of political beliefs—what ideas get sorted into the red or blue box—is not universal or enduring, but is formed by the events of the last Summer, by the 1960s. In the last saeculum the constellation was different. We may, for example, presume that pro-women's rights and pro-immigration are in the same box, but in the last saeculum, they were in different boxes. Our example, my Great-Aunt Maude, was born at the very end of the Missionary Generation, the very end of the Spring that began the saeculum, a point analogous to someone born in about 1958 in our current saeculum. Most of her life was spent in the ideological constellation of the previous one. By the 1970s this made no sense to her young nieces and nephews, just as the cultural constellations of the Baby Boomers will make no sense to young people in 2038!

Now let's take the next piece of it. The Temperance Movement peaked with Missionary women and with the passage of the Eighteenth Amendment and the establishment of Prohibition in 1920, and then crashed after the repeal of Prohibition in 1932, ultimately ceasing to be an important issue in American politics after 1945. The coalitions fell apart, abandoned in droves by Lost Generation women.

---

15. Riiko Bedford, "Heredity as Ideology: Ideas of the Woman's Christian Temperance Union of the United States and Ontario on Heredity and Social Reform, 1880–1910," *Canada Bulletin of Medical History* 32, no. 1 (Spring 2015): 77–100, https://www.utpjournals.press/doi/pdf/10.3138/cbmh.32.1.77.

My granny (Great-Aunt Maude's younger sister) and my Great-Aunt Helen were Lost Generation, not Missionary. They had completely different attitudes about nearly everything—wild, daring, complicated, and dangerous. My granny believed in psychic phenomena and was a subject at the Rhine Institute in the 1930s, traveled far from her hometown, and helped refugees at a displaced persons camp in Germany after the war. My Great-Aunt Helen married a doctor and moved to the coalfields of West Virginia in the 1930s. She had some amazing stories and scandalized the family by wearing a bikini in her sixties and going water skiing for her seventieth birthday. They drank, smoked, took the name of the Lord in vain, and believed in ghosts and "the Sight" in the blood of their Scottish ancestors. They loved their sister, but she was stuffy and righteous in their opinion. "That's just Maude," was what my granny said. Not for one minute would either of them have joined the Temperance Movement, embraced birth control as a means of eugenics for controlling the poor, or marched for the rights of women. Their idea of a strong woman was Amelia Earhart, not Susan B. Anthony.

And there we see the divide between Missionary and Lost! As you take apart what seem like simple memories, you will learn a great deal about how these cycles work. You will discover tremendous complexities and apparent contradictions—parts of your story that you may see in an entirely new light. Write these things down. Take notes. Learn about the context of what you remember. Also, remember that you do not have to be talking about a blood relative. You are talking about the oldest person you personally have known, whoever that person is. This is your method of finding your way into the history of the last saeculum and into last Winter.

Stories as Messages

Once you have begun to unpack the stories of the oldest people you have personally known, it's time to consider the stories of people you don't personally know. Recording oral history is important because it preserves the stories of people whose stories are otherwise lost—usually because they aren't considered important enough for some reason. There are biographies of generals and presidents, celebrities and superstars; overwhelmingly, biographies are about people who are rich and powerful. They are not about people who did important things, who preserved their communities or served others but did not achieve great fame. They are not about people who influenced and protected and nurtured rather than achieved great wealth. They are most often about white men with a lot of money. Oral history seeks to record the stories of everyone else: of the common soldier rather than the general, of the teacher rather than the president, of the priest rather than the millionaire, of the doctor rather than the world-famous scientist. We need those stories, the stories of people like us who survived last Winter and made the world a better place.

Many universities have collections of oral histories of the Great Depression and the Second World War, but most are not readily accessible to the general reader. One very good pair of books that invite the reader to hear the own-voices stories of people who lived then are *Hard Times* and *The Good War* by Studs Terkel. According to the *New York Times*, *Hard Times* "is known for providing an equal representation of experiences across a broad spectrum of socioeconomic status."[16] *Hard Times* tells the story of the Great Depression through relating the stories of people who lived then in their own words.[17] *The Good War* does the same for World War II, broadening the canvas to include not just American voices but the perspectives of people on the other side as well. It covers not just soldiers in wartime but the experiences of people at home, both those who suffered because of the war and those who profited from it. It's an ideal beginning point to read oral history because the stories are short, personal, and varied—almost anyone can find someone from a community that they are part of represented.[18]

So why do this? Because the best way to understand Winter is to hear about the experiences of people who lived through the last Winter. Since the cycle of the saeculum is eighty years long, most of the people who lived through the years 1925–1945 are dead and we cannot ask them to tell us their

---

16. Adam Cohen, "Studs Terkel's Legacy: A Vivid Window on the Great Depression" *New York Times*, November 8, 2008, https://www.nytimes.com/2008/11/08/opinion/08sat4.html.

17. Studs Terkel, *Hard Times* (New York: Pantheon Press, 1970).

18. Studs Terkel, *The Good War* (New York: Ballantine Books, 1984).

stories or give us advice. However, we can read the stories they left behind. We can absorb the lore of our people through their words.

And, fortunately, we can also absorb their voices and narratives by other means as well. The movies and music of the time give us tremendous insight into what people liked, what they thought, and what they hoped for. For example, many movies of the 1930s were rags-to-riches stories where a deserving person became wealthy, allowing the glamorous sets and costumes and travel presented to the viewer to be guilt-free. After all, the viewer could revel in the luxury suddenly given to someone who deserved it rather than wallow in the excess belonging to those who clearly didn't. One could imagine oneself the recipient of so many nice things along with the protagonist.

Perhaps the single best own-voices movie made about World War II, made at the time by the people who lived it rather than by others or in reflection decades later, is *The Best Years of Our Lives*.[19] It tells the story of three veterans coming home after the war to find that their families have changed while they were gone, and so have they. It won seven Academy Awards, including Best Supporting Actor for Harold Russell, a double amputee playing a double amputee, one of the first veterans to be so realistically portrayed.[20] If you are able, find *The Best Years of Our Lives* and watch it, as it will give you an incredible perspective on the end of the war.

There are many excellent autobiographies about the Great Depression and World War II, far too many to list here, but you are encouraged to seek some that speak to you or that record the lives of people belonging to a group you identify with. For example, the excellent biography of Charles McGee, one of the Tuskegee Airmen, written by his daughter, provides a look both at growing up in the Depression and then of the war.[21] If you are seeking queer history, Allan Berube's *Coming Out Under Fire* contains interviews with dozens of gay and lesbian veterans of World War II.[22] Take the opportunity to explore the experience of your folk in the last Winter, however you define

---

19. William Wyler, *The Best Years of Our Lives* (MGM, 1946), film, 170 min.

20. Harold Russell, *Victory in My Hands* (New York: Creative Age Press, 1949).

21. Charlene E. McGee Smith, *Tuskegee Airman* (Boston: Branden Publishing Company, 2001).

22. Allan Bérubé, *Coming Out under Fire* (New York: Macmillan, 1990).

your folk. That may mean blood kin, or that may mean folk who align with your own identity.

But some will ask, what if my family weren't in the United States before 1945? What if, for example, your family emigrated from India as a result of Partition? Your family's story is part of this too. Why your family came here, what was happening to them in the thirties and forties, and what happened when they arrived is a unique part of the American tale. If we all put our stories together, we would have a vast and intricate patchwork quilt of stories, each square different from the one beside it. Some would seem ordinary and others extraordinary, but each one would be unique. There is no correct narrative, whether your family's experience was in the mainstream or was an exception. Perhaps your family was rich in the Great Depression! Perhaps nobody in your family was impacted by World War II. The stories of minority experiences are also important.

Or perhaps your stories are lost. Your father was adopted in 1950, given up by an unknown mother. Perhaps you, yourself, came to America as an orphan from Cambodia, a child from a refugee camp fleeing the Khmer Rouge. You don't know the full story. But it's still there. The gods know, and the story is written in your blood. You are the story. You are the victory. You can't read the book, but the last page says, "And then one day the child of that child sat down and they wondered." The mystery is part of the tapestry.

That's why in our next rite we will honor those who came before, those who survived harsh Winter in their own time so that we could know the time after. From them, we will draw wisdom to sustain us in this present Winter. Our ancestors, whether our literal ancestors or those of our people who have gone before, have much wisdom that they can still share with us. In the next rite, we'll explore a Roman ritual for asking for ancestral guidance.

The Roman Parentalia

Roman funeral customs were complex—as one might expect from an empire that stretched from the British Isles to Syria and encompassed many peoples—and there were many variations over a time span of hundreds of years. However, some customs were widespread; one of which was the making of funeral masks.

When a Roman died at home peacefully and surrounded by family, a wax death mask was often made. This was done by painting the person's face with melted wax until the wax had built up and dried enough so that it could be carefully removed, creating a mask of that person's face that looked as they had at their time of death. This served as a last remembrance of them for their family. Often the mask was added to the household shrine or hung on the wall behind images of the gods. Offerings were put in front of it and it was the focus of mourning and remembrance. If the family was wealthy enough, they could have a sturdier copy made in bronze. Some families also had copies made in clay. In Roman Egypt, where wax would not hold up well in a hot climate, a funeral portrait might have been painted instead. If the family was very distinguished, they could have a sculptor copy the likeness in marble.[23]

The mask would watch over the family as a loving ancestor, and the collection of family masks was the focus of an annual rite in honor of the dead: the Parentalia. In some ways, the Parentalia may be the distant forebearer of the Day of the Dead as it is now practiced in the New World. Of course there were no photographs, but the masks filled much the same role. On February 13 at dawn, the festival would begin with a libation to honor the dead. The household shrine would be lit with lamps and decked with flowers. Later in the day the family would visit the graves of loved ones and bring offerings.[24] Ovid says, "The spirits who live below are not greedy. A tile wreathed in garlands, a sprinkling of grain, a few grains of salt, bread soaked in wine, and some loose violets—these are offerings enough."[25] The honored ancestors were asked to give their blessings to the living and were regarded as sources of wisdom and comfort—loving great-grandparents to help, not dangerous spirits to be appeased.

---

23. Jane Fejfer, *Roman Portraits in Context* (Berlin: Walter de Gruyter, 2009), 175–176.

24. Frances Bernstein, *Classical Living* (San Francisco: Harper San Francisco, 2000).

25. Ovid, *The Fasti* (New York: Penguin Classics, 2004).

Some well-known people were honored by those who were not just their descendants. It can be argued that the idea of public statues as memorials to important dead people was an extension of the funeral mask to the public sphere rather than just the private. While we think of these as being statues of emperors and generals, there were many sculptures and effigies that were not. For example, in the Roman city of Perge, there is a series of inscriptions in honor of a woman named Plancia Magna, who was both the highest civil servant (a.k.a. the mayor) and the High Priestess of Artemis. She was also apparently a Jew who had converted to Paganism, wife of a senator, and the mother of several children. The wording and stature of her inscriptions make her the mother of the city, an ancestor invoked by those who lived there whether or not they were her literal descendants.[26]

A Modern Parentalia Rite

If you do not wish to call on your actual ancestors in the following rite, please feel free to choose someone you revere as the mother of your city, a real person who is dead and who is the parent of your folk.

The date for the Roman Parentalia is February 13, but you may also choose a day appropriate for honoring the dead in your tradition. For example, you may prefer to do this at Samhain if that seems appropriate to you. If you prefer, you may also choose a new moon, as the dark of the moon is a time for reaching out to the dead in many traditions.

Making the Masks

First, we will make the ancestral masks. You may make one or several as you wish. Each one should represent a person you revere and whose counsel you seek for the coming Winter, someone who survived such times and therefore has good advice to impart. Remember that you are asking this person for advice and that the advice you receive is the advice they would have given you

---

26. Barbara F. McManus, "Plancia Magna, Aurelia Paulina, and Regilla: Civic Donors," Vroma .org, retrieved May 16, 2019, http://www.vroma.org/~bmcmanus/women_civicdonors .html.

in life. If you don't think Granddad would have given you advice you want to hear, don't ask him for it!

If you are so skilled, you may fashion the masks by hand out of clay; however, most people will find it easier to work with a premade form.

You will need:
full-face mask forms, either paper or plastic (these are readily available at
    craft stores in the autumn or online all year round)
paint (if you have a plastic form, check that the paint will adhere to plastic)
brushes/painting implements
sequins, beads, feathers, or other ornaments if you like
glue to attach ornaments
craft paper or tissue paper for decoupage if you desire

Once you have your mask form and decorating materials, consider how to best render the person you intend to honor. You may paint the mask realistically as a representation of them, using paint and ornaments to make a portrait. You may choose to be more abstract, using craft or tissue paper to decoupage things that remind you of them—for example, pictures of fishing, fishing rods, fish, boats, waterfowl, and lakes for a grandfather who was an avid fisherman and outdoorsman. You may choose to be more abstract still, making a portrait of their spirit as you perceive it—an animal, a color combination, a repeating design that has meaning. You may ornament the masks any way you wish, embellishing them with beads, sequins, seashells, found objects—whatever adds to this portrait.

Once you have completed your mask or masks, allow them to sit overnight somewhere they will not be disturbed to give time for the paint or glue to dry. Depending on how complex your design is, you may need to work on the mask over several sessions, allowing it to dry completely between sessions. Then you are ready for the rite.

The Rite
You will need:
the mask(s) you have made

appropriate flowers (see below)

a white candle

a dish of salt

bread

a cup of wine or the beverage of your choice (see below)

The wine is an offering to the ancestors you call upon, so it can be a different beverage if you find that appropriate. If Granddad never touched wine in his life and definitely preferred Kentucky Bourbon, you may certainly substitute! Likewise, if Aunt Mary was never seen without her red label Coca-Cola, you may use that instead.

Flowers are a traditional offering for the ancestors. As we saw in the previous quote from Ovid, violets were preferred. However, violets only blossom for a very short time in the spring, and it's possible that they will not be available. You may use an African violet in a pot as a substitute. Other possibilities include using a flower that has associations with the dead in another culture. For example, white chrysanthemums are used for funerals and grave offerings in Japan, while marigolds are associated with the Day of the Dead in Mexico and the Southwestern United States. Or you may use a flower that you particularly associate with an ancestor you mean to honor. For example, many veterans have red, white, and blue flowers at their funerals. Another example: my maternal grandmother loved blue hydrangeas and I never see them without thinking of her. What kind of flower you choose is ultimately up to you.

Optional extras:

mementos or symbols appropriate to the person(s) whose mask you have
    made

symbols of divinity in your tradition

Beginning the Rite

Remember, the purpose of this is to honor the ancestors and ask for their counsel as people who have lived through this season of Winter. They do not need to be your literal ancestors. They can be mentors or spiritual ancestors—the guiding lights of your folk, however you define them. Also remember that the counsel you will get from them is the counsel you would have received from them in life. In other words, if you don't want to talk to your mother, don't pick up the phone and call her! Call upon people whose wisdom you wish to receive, not people with whom you had contentious relationships or who you think did not make good decisions or give good advice.

If you have a permanent altar in your home, you may choose to hang the masks on the wall behind it, or you may lay them out or present them on the altar. In Roman homes, there was often a wall niche where the masks of the ancestors lived with just enough space beneath to put a few offerings. The top of a bookcase or a high shelf is appropriate. If you do not wish to keep the masks up and only wish to use them at certain seasons or for certain rites, put them above an altar temporarily and store them safely afterward. If you do not have a permanent altar, set one up on a table or other surface for the duration of the rite and then put it away afterward.

Arrange the masks so that they look upon your offerings, the wine or its substitute, the bit of bread and salt, and the flowers you have chosen. Place the white candle in front, being careful to put it where it will not set the masks or any ornaments on fire, and light it. Speak directly to the masks. "Departed ones, *name and name*, I honor you today. In your lives you lived through many hard times. In your lives you survived the season of Winter. Now Winter has come again. I ask for your wise counsel. What are the best ways to navigate these waters? How do I come through this as you did? What advice can you give me? I ask as one who admires you, as one who loves you. Please help me to know what to do."

Close your eyes and visualize the person as clearly as you can. Speak to them, either aloud or mentally, telling them your fears and hopes, telling them about the situation you find yourself in this Winter, and perhaps recalling something of what they did. For example, if you know that your chosen person traveled many miles to find safety or employment, remember that. If you know they fought against Fascism, liberated a concentration camp, or died in the South Pacific, remember that. If you know they survived a hardscrabble childhood as an orphan in the Great Depression, remember that.

Recall their experiences and their heroism. Talk to them. Pour out your worries and your desires. Then listen. You may feel nothing. Or you may feel a sense of peace or simply the sense that someone is listening. You will probably not feel that you have an answer to your questions in this moment. Even honored ancestors usually need to think! Thank them for their attention.

Extinguish the candle but leave the offerings before them overnight if that is possible. The next day, pour the wine, bread, and salt outdoors. Leave the masks where they are for a few days if you can, until you have received the advice you sought.

Listening for Counsel

Over the following days, listen for the counsel you have requested. Perhaps you will suddenly remember a story about the person that you thought you had forgotten. Perhaps a new story will come to light. Maybe you'll be listening to the radio and a song will come on that speaks to you—perhaps a song they knew or loved, or perhaps just something that speaks with their voice. Maybe you'll suddenly see a billboard, a literal sign, that directs you. Maybe someone will unexpectedly say something that reminds you sharply of your ancestor. Maybe you'll find a book they loved and in it find a message that inspired them. Or perhaps you'll literally hear their voice behind you: words of encouragement or wisdom.

When you feel that you have heard the advice you requested, thank the ancestors you have invoked once again. You may simply thank them verbally, or you may repeat your offerings of bread, salt, wine, or flowers.

For the Romans, the Parentalia altars stayed up for nine days, from February 13 to February 21, when the public festival of the Feralia began and the doors to the otherworld were officially closed and the ancestors returned to the land beneath.[27] If you have done your rite on February 13, you may mark the end of the Parentalia by putting the masks away on February 21. If you have chosen another date, expect the answer to the counsel you requested within nine days. After that time, thank the ancestors and put away the masks until next year.

---

27. Bernstein, *Classical Living*, 45–46.

The Crisis Approaches

····· Chapter 4 ·····

Last Winter—
Broadening the Picture

As we consider our stories, let's review how last Winter played out. Our last Winter had three phases that we will look at in greater depth:

The Cold Arrives: circa 1925–1932

Days without Sun: 1933–1941

The Blizzard: 1942–1945

The Cold Arrives: Circa 1925–1932

In 1925 the United States was enjoying an unprecedented economic boom. Industrialization had grown the economy, and the results of World War I had been economic stagnation and damage to infrastructure in Europe, which had the temporary effect of shutting European goods out of international markets. As Britain, France, and Germany reeled from their losses, the United States had a tremendous opportunity. After all, none of World War I had been fought on American soil, and while roughly 2.8 million served overseas, American casualties were light compared to those of our allies. Around fifty-eight thousand American soldiers were killed in action, while the British suffered more than seven hundred thousand killed in action[28] and the French lost more than a million.[29] For those Americans who served in the trenches in France, like my paternal grandfather, the war was a life-altering experience. However, it was also comparatively rare. Being a veteran of the Great War made one a member of an exclusive club, and there was the sense among those veterans that most people could never understand what they had been through or what modern warfare was like. They organized in groups like the American Legion, whose initial mission was to require the government to provide ongoing healthcare for veterans after they left the service, including support for amputations and chronic health problems resulting from wounds or chemical warfare. In this way, the impacts of World War I on American society were much like the effects of the wars in Iraq and Afghanistan in the next saeculum—they loomed larger than their actual physical impacts and contributed to a sharp cultural divide between those who fought the war and those who reaped the resulting economic benefits.

But many more things were happening than the fallout from World War I. In the earlier part of the saeculum, in the Summer era at the turn of the century, education for women, women's rights, and suffrage had come to the fore as major issues. The founding of many women's colleges meant an explosion in the number of young women who had access to postsecondary education. While some women did go to college earlier, it was an elite opportunity reserved for a few. The founding of literally dozens around the turn of the century meant that Lost Generation women (born between 1885 and 1905) attended college in unprecedented numbers. This created a social class of educated women who could work at white-collar jobs, who earned their own wages without being dependent on a male relative, and who embraced a sophisticated definition of independence. While of course women had always worked, most had been employed in factories, as domestic help, or in other low-status jobs in the late nineteenth century. (This was not true

28. "Viewpoint: 10 Big Myths about World War One Debunked," BBC News, February 25, 2014, https://www.bbc.com/news/magazine-25776836.

29. Michel Huber, *La Population de la France Pendant la Guerre* (Paris: Les Presses Universitaires de France, 1931).

earlier in the century, or in the eighteenth century, but there was a Victorian backlash that we tend to think of as the status of all women prior to the turn of the century, when in actuality it was simply the previous phase.) However, the ending of this phase and the opportunity for women's education created a new ideal—the Flapper.

The Flapper lived on her own not because she had to but because she wanted to. Whether that was in a (gasp) boarding house or with friends, she had her own place that she paid for. She drove an automobile, thereby rendering her comings and goings free from parental interference. She spent her own money on her own clothing, purchasing or making things in a style that her elders would certainly not approve of—short skirts, stockings held above the knee with fancy garters that showed when she walked or sat, and "combinations": a one-piece silk or cotton undergarment with no boning or stays, just a connected camisole and panty. She listened to the radio, pulling in hot songs from across the country. Most importantly, the Flapper was perceived as being sexually free. After all, there was no one to police her chastity! Who knew what she might be doing?

Of course as with any ideal, most women didn't live the full lifestyle touted as the new big thing. My granny had attended a women's college for two years when she met a veteran five years her senior—a man who was (scandalously) divorced—and dropped out of school to marry him. A picture from the time shows her with the bobbed haircut that was the Flapper signature, and certainly she danced the Charleston and went to jazz clubs and drank despite Prohibition, but she was not a young single lady in the big city. She was a young married woman with a baby boy born in 1924, and her job was keeping the books at a company owned by her husband and brother. And yet she certainly considered herself a Flapper, a part of the social movement away from Victorian morality.

In the 1920s there was a sense that society was reeling. New technologies had emerged that contributed to enormous social mobility as well as physical mobility. For example, the ubiquity of rail travel to almost everywhere in the United States meant that immigrant populations no longer had to cluster in seaport cities but could move to where the work was. This meant there was enormous cultural disruption as monocultural rural areas suddenly experienced an influx of people from an entirely different culture. My maternal grandfather, then a high school principal in a small town in upstate New York, struggled when half the students were suddenly Catholic immigrants from Southern Italy—a big change in a town previously rock-ribbed WASP like something out of a play by Thornton Wilder. Anti-immigrant sentiment ran high, only instead of the immigrants being Spanish-speaking and from Central America, as they were in the 2000s, they were Italian-speaking and from Sicily.

Sometime in the 1920s, Autumn turned to Winter. Exactly which event marked the transition is something historians continue to debate. Did Winter begin with the rise of Mussolini, the first of the Fascist dictators, in 1922? With the election of Herbert Hoover as president in 1928? With the stock market crash in 1929? As with many seasonal transitions in the great year, no one single moment marked the shift. Cultural change is gradual. A new technology emerges, but not everyone rushes out to buy it the day it becomes available! New technologies slowly penetrate, becoming more common until they are ubiquitous. The same is true of cultural touchstones—for example, in the 1920s, movie houses became common in American cities and towns, bringing the latest Hollywood movies to even very rural areas and creating a new widespread media culture. By 1930, moviegoers were buying ninety-five million tickets per week.[30] Also by 1930, "talkies," movies with sound, were replacing silent films, making going to the movies even more attractive. However, people didn't all decide to go to the movies every week one day in 1927! Gradually, over a decade, going to the movies became easier and more common across the country.

Likewise, the increase in crime in the 1920s didn't happen overnight. The murder rate rose 78 percent between 1920 and 1933, reaching a level nearly twice the murder rate in 2015. The prison population increased by 361 per-

---

30. "Let's Go to the Movies: The Mechanics of Moving Images," Moah.org, retrieved May 18, 2019. http://www.moah.org/movies/movie_theatres_p.html.

cent.[31] This was a gradual change across the period, not a sudden leap in response to a single event. People were in truth living in a more dangerous world, and the rising sense of fear was based on actual events.

The economy crashed in October 1929 when the stock market tanked over a period of several days, losing more than $30 billion in value, or $92.1 billion in 2017 dollars. This kicked off the Great Depression, the greatest economic problem the United States has ever known, and ruined not only individual investors but pension funds, insurance companies, and banks themselves. Many small banks closed, their customers losing all their money permanently. (There was no FDIC then, because it was created in response to this crisis.) It is not exaggeration to say that millions of individuals and families were completely financially ruined.

The results of the crash continued to spin out over the next few years. For example, my maternal grandfather was an elementary school principal in 1929 and my grandmother was a fourth grade teacher. They were not initially impacted. However, the next year the town could not collect enough taxes to keep the schools open and had to lay off most of the school personnel. Both of their jobs ceased to exist at the same time as the elementary schools simply didn't open in the fall of 1930. Like so many others, they migrated to find work, a family with a young child moving from relative to relative, seeking permanent employment.

Meanwhile, a few miles away, my paternal grandparents faced the same problem. My grandfather and great-uncle's business went bankrupt for lack of customers, putting them and my grandmother all out of a job at once. Their house was foreclosed on. Things that had been bought on credit were repossessed. My grandfather found temporary work as a night shift security guard, then a bunch of short jobs as a salesman for various businesses. He also took up bootlegging. Crime pays, and in the Great Depression, people did what they had to do.

You have stories like this too. Maybe you know them. Maybe you don't. But they are there. The entire United States went through an enormous economic

---

31. Tim Nash, "Organized Crime in the 1920's and Prohibition," The Finer Times, February, November 23, 2008, https://www.thefinertimes.com/organised-crime-in-the-1920s.

convulsion. From 1929 to 1932, millions of people were displaced or financially ruined. Winter had come with a bang.

Days without Sun: 1933–1941

In November 1932, Franklin Delano Roosevelt was elected president of the United States. Ten weeks later, Hitler became chancellor of Germany. In early 1933, the stage was set for the conflicts to come.

And yet at the time few people thought that either development was a game-changer. Yes, a Democratic challenger had limited unpopular Republican President Hoover to one term. Yes, Hitler was a populist demagogue who preached anti-Semitism and encouraged the worst impulses of radical right-wing groups. But neither of these developments appeared outside the framework of "normal" in 1933. It was only as their policies began to take effect, leading two nations in opposite directions in response to the global financial crisis, that the storm clouds on the northern horizon darkened to such a degree that ignoring them became impossible.

Throughout the middle 1930s, most Americans were focused on personally surviving the Great Depression. Roosevelt's policies were slow to take effect, and there were calls for revolution from both right and left. We forget that both Fascism and Communism had organized political support in the 1930s, and that both Hitler and Stalin sought to destabilize the United States and encourage a new government aligned with Germany or Russia. We are no longer aware of the level of polarization, of the clashes between various groups in American life, of the hatreds that were fomented then. Most people who lived through this time wanted to forget. They wanted to remember great movies, warm family relationships, or childhoods made happy by parents who tried so hard to protect them—not lynchings, massive marches against one group or another, and the fear that spread like a miasma beneath the surface. Something was wrong. Something was very wrong, and it was only possible to ignore it for so long. We don't remember because those who were there wanted to forget.

Thomas Hobbes, the English political theorist, called this state "the war of all against all," arguing that people don't organize politically in favor of something or to pursue some positive goal, but out of fear of others. Fear and violence, he argues in *Leviathan*, are natural. The normal state of human existence is for peoples to seek to destroy one another based on memberships in different tribes, and that truly every group is perpetually at war with every other group. Sometimes, temporarily, this state of affairs may be interrupted, either by the strength of some overwhelming overlord, or by constructing a social contract that imposes peace. Hobbes was in favor of these social contracts but doubted that any contract could constrain humanity's natural impulses to hurt those who are different for very long.[32] In the 1930s it seemed that the rational systems of the previous century had been utterly destroyed and that the war of all against all was unleashed—rich against poor, Christians against Jews, white against black, women against men, and so on. Every conceivable division was to the fore, and every fight was to the death. Losers would literally burn.

How do you live in a world like that? Those who were alive at the time had to come to an answer. They had to find ways to survive and thrive. For some, the answer was family, and for others, work. For some it was spirituality and personal peace. For others it was taking up arms. For some, it was craft, and for others, the pursuit of law and justice.

Some failed. Some died. Some gave up. Some decided that the only thing that mattered was getting rich on the spoils. Winter tests everyone and it separates the gold from the base metal. Understanding the stories of people who lived then can show us how they faced the crisis and help us make conscious choices about whose paths we wish to emulate.

As the 1930s drew to a close, war raged in Europe and Asia both. On July 7, 1937, Japan invaded China. On September 1, 1939, German troops invaded Poland, beginning World War II. Americans watched nervously. Many advocated "America First," staying out of all foreign wars. Some wanted to intervene on the part of allies like Britain, France, and China, while others were sympathetic to Germany or Japan. Most feared what would happen if the United States became embroiled in these struggles. Some denied this

---

32. Thomas Hobbes, *Leviathan* (New York: Penguin Classics, 2017).

was possible, still saying that there would be no major war even as the conflicts escalated. The internal war of all against all reached a crescendo with radio personalities exhorting listeners to one side or another, marches of German-American Bund supporters in major cities, and threats to assassinate President Roosevelt from the Silver Legion.[33] What decision would the United States make?

On December 7, 1941, the question was answered when the Japanese bombed the American naval base at Pearl Harbor in Hawaii, killing 2,335 American soldiers, sailors, and airmen as well as sixty-eight Hawaiian civilians.[34] The next day the United States entered World War II. The storm had broken.

The Blizzard: 1942–1945

What can we say about a crisis that touched almost every person living in the United States at the time? How can we imagine the scope? More than sixteen million Americans served in World War II, about 11 percent of the total population. (This number does not count women who worked in war material factories, men in the merchant marine, or many other civilian jobs that were directly involved with the war effort.) Given that half the population was over 50 or under 10, and that of the other half many were teenagers, mothers of young children, or unable to serve because of their health, nearly every possible young man served. Nearly half a million were killed, if you include merchant sailors killed at sea.

Each of those people had parents, children, brothers and sisters, friends, lovers—every single person who lived through these years knew many who fought and some who died. Everyone had stories. My Great-Uncle Bill, then a small-town policeman on the Carolina coast, was too old to serve, and told the story of a friend's son lost at sea when his ship was torpedoed. The Graveyard of the Atlantic was kind; his body washed up on the beach and

---

33. Mel Ayton, *Hunting the President* (New York: Regnery History Press, 2014).

34. "Frequently Asked Questions about Pearl Harbor—How Many People Died at Pearl Harbor during the Attack?" Visitpearlharbor.org, retrieved May 18, 2019, https://visitpearlharbor.org/faqs-questions-pearl-harbor/.

was found by his elementary school teacher, allowing his parents to know what happened and bury him properly rather than wonder and mourn at an empty grave. My mother, graduating from high school in 1944, watched every boy in her class but one go to war right after graduation. Many never returned. And my father was in combat for 180 days, from the Normandy Breakout to the Rhine Crossing.

You have stories. You may know them. You may have listened to them when you were a child, asked for them as a teenager, or even dreaded hearing people tell them. Remember them. Some of them are terrifying and some are boring. Some are "you had to be there" kinds of stories. Some make you uncomfortable. Think about them. Pull them out of the back corner of your mind and examine them again.

Or maybe you don't know the stories. Maybe something has interrupted the transmission of lore. You never heard them. They're still there. There are many ways to research the lives of people who lived such a short time ago, to reclaim the birthright of a story that is yours. If you can, and there are those of your folk who are still living, take this opportunity to ask for their stories and record them. In the next decade, the last people with adult memories of World War II will be gone. It will be too late to ask for their stories then.

Why does it matter? It matters because the stories of the momentous events of the last Winter are the keys to navigating this Winter. We are sailing in what is for us uncharted waters, dangerous waters filled with treacherous shoals. We need the maps that tell us what currents run here, the astronomical observations that teach us the pattern of the tides, and the portulary that will bring us to harbor. We have not sailed these waters before, but those who came before us did. They lived through Winter. Their stories can guide us.

The years 1942–1945 brought momentous changes. Aside from those who fought the war, enormous changes happened that touched everyone at home, from the growth of industrial jobs that finally allowed employment to rebound from the Great Depression, to women entering the paid workplace at unprecedented levels, to the undermining of barriers like segregation. For a lot of people these years were a hold-onto-your-socks time, a roller coaster of bad and good that upended their lives. By the end of 1945, the world was forever changed, and so were they.

A Rite in the Style of the Previous Winter

As we talked about in the last chapter, there was a flourishing magical community in the last Winter. As is true of the magical community today, it was very diverse. A number of elements went into it:

- Folkways of particular ethnic groups, from Native American, to Afro-Caribbean, to various European and Asian beliefs. Some of those folkways were very ancient, and some were syncretic and evolving.
- Spiritualist beliefs popularized by the various teachers and organizations in the Spiritualist Movement of the early 1900s.
- Offshoots of the Golden Dawn and the many American Lodges that formed either as descendants of Golden Dawn traditions or were inspired by them.
- Psychic research and "scientific magic" based on the new field of parapsychology exemplified by the Rhine Institute.
- Neopagan groups that sought to re-create ancient (mostly Classical) rites like the Church of Aphrodite on Long Island.
- Revealed doctrine books purporting to explain the secret teachings of Ascended Masters, usually from Tibet or East Asia. Many of these were part of correspondence courses offered by individual teachers.

As is true of the magical community today, many people who had an interest in spiritual, occult, and magical things had knowledge of and affiliation with more than one of these threads. Books proliferated, allowing ideas to cross-pollinate from one tradition to another, reaching people who were not part of communities with a living tradition and inviting people from one group to expand their knowledge by learning about another group. There was the common Universalist thread to much of this—the idea that all of these pieces were part of a greater whole, and that each individual seed held a truth. The Missionary Generation had a drive toward syncretism—that by assembling all the disparate pieces, the greater truth could be learned. The Lost Generation tended to be more prosaic—if it works, do it.

Of course each individual's experience was different. Some remained solidly within one tradition and some sampled eclectically. One thing which may surprise us today is the strong tradition of Christian magic: the idea that there was no conflict between being a good Christian and using "God-given" gifts for the betterment of humanity. This was a core principle of many of the Universalists. My paternal grandmother certainly considered herself a strong Lutheran. To her, having the Sight or going to séances or speaking with the dead would have been simply using a gift. The gift was neither good nor bad. What you chose to do with it was moral or immoral. Using it to harm others was wrong, just as using the gift of superior strength to punch people was wrong. In fact, many of the models specifically invoke Christian theology in magical ritual with Psalms, Bible verses, and angelic invocations.

As Winter deepened, so too did the desire to know what the future held. In uncertain times people crave guidance or want to "lift the veil" and get a hint of what is going to happen. As a result, there were many forms of divination popularized, especially tarot cards. Tarot had been around a long time—since the fifteenth century by some accounts—and decks had been commercially available since the Tarot of Marseille in the late eighteenth century. However, the Rider-Waite deck, with its beautiful illustrations by Pamela Colman Smith and its accompanying guidebook, was published in 1909 and rapidly became the most popular and readily available deck.[35] By the late 1920s it was widely known as a divination method in the United States, whether for "fortune-telling" at bazaars and fairs, or in earnest. A large part of its success was that it was easy to use. Unlike pendulum dowsing or scrying, which required either affinity or a great deal of practice, or bibliomancy, which required faith in the Bible, or many other methods that required instruction from a teacher to learn, the Rider-Waite tarot came with instructions and has been beginner-friendly ever since. You don't need a personal

---

35. Place, *The Tarot*.

teacher and you don't need extensive practice to gain anything useful from it. It's perfectly possible to buy the deck and the book and get to work.

The following is a ritual constructed around using a tarot deck for divination in the style of the 1930s. Again, what individuals and groups actually did then is as varied as it is now, but this gives a good glimpse of the style of the time, written for a modern group to enact. This is a community-based ritual, but if you are alone, you can adapt as needed to your situation. Some notes before we begin:

- You do not have to use the Rider-Waite deck for this, though it is most appropriate. Use whatever deck you prefer and are familiar with.
- This ritual cuts down the focus on energy work, polarity, and familiarity with your ruling element and astrological sign because most modern groups don't use these concepts as extensively. However, the concepts are introduced because they are critical to the structure of the ritual.

Today, we tend to think of polarity as being about male and female rather than about projection versus reception of energy; however, this concept emerged in circles that were mostly or exclusively male in the nineteenth century and was not about physical gender characteristics to begin with. It was only late in the century, in the era of the Golden Dawn, when the idea emerged that women's energy, still perceived as inherently different from men's, was necessary to a balanced circle. Prior to that period, most Lodges had been exclusively male, and polarity had nothing to do with the biological sex of the participants.

What emerged was the ideal of a circle that perfectly balanced male and female energies as well as elemental affinities. The ideal circle would have six heterosexual couples: six men and six women paired off, each man a projective fire or air sign, and each woman a receptive water or earth sign. This almost never existed in practicality. In real life then, as today, you and your friends don't sort that neatly. Real groups seated to create energy balance with the people they had, and this was often far from the recommendation. You do not have to try to re-create the ideal—almost nobody ever had it to begin with, and they all did perfectly well without. In practice, the important thing is to balance the energy so that it rests lightly in the hands of the officiant, each person contributing to the group's desire in a way that is harmonious and easy to direct. That balance has nothing to do with anyone's physical gender.

However, you do need to know people's astrological signs. Here is a chart showing what a person's elemental affinity is based on their sun sign:

Air	Fire	Water	Earth
Aquarius	Aries	Pisces	Capricorn
Gemini	Leo	Cancer	Taurus
Libra	Sagittarius	Scorpio	Virgo

However, the sun sign is not the only important influence in a chart, and without going into a long and technical discussion of astrology, just bear in mind that sometimes the other influences in a chart are more important to an individual than their sun sign. If somebody is a Sagittarius and says they actually have an affinity with water, go with that.

To seat the circle you will need at least four people, one on each of the elemental quarters. Ideally, each quarter should be held by someone with an affinity for that element. Decide who will be doing each quarter, and then if you have more than four people, put them between the quarters in a balanced way. In other words, if you have a fiery Aries and a fiery Leo, don't put them next to each other. Put an earth or water between them if possible.

This ritual is written for two leaders. In theory, the priest is the projective air or fire person who will lead from South, while the priestess is the receptive water or earth person who will do the divination from North. In practice, then as now, things varied considerably. Let's take the example of my grandparents from the last chapter. My grandmother was a very projective, high-energy Leo and my grandfather was a receptive, "psychic" Scorpio. She would have led off South and he would have done the divination from North, essentially switching the roles. Also, he would be switching off his natural quarter of West to North in order to better balance the circle. When we read or hear about the very rigid rules in this style, bear in mind that they illustrated the principles, and that in real life people adapted generously. Thus, rather than use the terms "priest" and "priestess" for the two officiants, we will use "warden" and "reader" to reflect their function in the circle.

You will need:

a table large enough for everyone to sit at, preferably round

chairs for everyone to sit at the table

a candleholder with five branches (like an Advent candleholder) or five votive cups that can be placed together

five candles (one yellow, red, blue, green, and white—tapers if you are using a candelabra or votives if you are using votive cups)

a ritual sword or knife

a deck of tarot cards

matches or a lighter

Optional extras:

a tablecloth with a mandala design or other symbols that speak to you

a compass if you do not know which way is north in the place you plan to do this

an ashtray if you are using matches

Set up the room with the table and chairs and tablecloth if you are using one. Use the compass to align the candelabra or votives to the directions so that the green candle is in the north, the yellow is in the east, the red is in the south, and blue is in the west. The white candle should be placed in the center. Put the matches or lighter and ashtray where they will be close at hand to the person sitting in the East chair. Put the sword or knife where it is in reach of the officiant who will be calling South and acting as warden. Put the tarot cards where they are in reach of the officiant who will be calling North and acting as reader. Turn out electrical lights so that the room is only dimly lit by the candles.

The Rite

Gather around the table. Each person should sit in their proper chair.

WARDEN: Take a moment to take a deep breath. Ground and center. Be here. [Pause while everyone does this, then nod to East to proceed.]

EASTERN QUARTER: Raphael, Angel of the East, of Morning and Spring, spread your protective wings over us and guide our sight, that we may seek true knowledge rather than deception. [You are not simply warding the space— you are also warding the reading. Light the yellow candle.]

SOUTHERN QUARTER/WARDEN: Michael, Angel of the South, of Day and Summer, spread your protective wings over us and guide our sight, that we may seek justice rather than advantage. [Light the red candle.]

WESTERN QUARTER: Gabriel, Angel of the West, of Evening and Autumn, spread your protective wings over us and guide our sight, that we may seek compassion rather than fortune. [Light the blue candle.]

NORTHERN QUARTER/READER: Uriel, Angel of the North, of Night and Winter, spread your protective wings over us and guide our sight, that we may seek wisdom rather than folly. [Light the green candle.]

WARDEN: Most High, Mighty Ones, grant us sanctity within this circle, that our work may be for the betterment of humanity and those assembled here, that we may better serve and guide, that we may act in accordance with the good. Let no deception enter here. Let no despair overtake us. Let no harm come to any as a result of these actions. So may it be. [Light the white candle. Unsheathe the blade. Progress *clockwise* around the circle, visualizing tracing a barrier of light around the outside, behind the chairs of everyone seated. When you return to your place, put the unsheathed blade on the table before you.]

READER: Let us join hands. [Each person takes the hand of the person on each side of them.] We are together. We feel each other's heartbeats. We hear each other's breaths. Pause, and listen. [Allow a moment of quiet, each person simply holding hands and feeling the energy of the circle. It may feel wonderful. It's a protected space, and if the energy is well-balanced it will be natural and pleasant. If the energy isn't well-balanced, the reader should try to even it out.]

WARDEN: [When enough time has elapsed] In days of old, the gods spoke through sibyls and prophets. We humbly ask for counsel, that we may use this knowledge to the good. [Ask the question. Some examples:

What will befall each of us in the coming months of crisis?

How may each of us best serve?

What should each of us be especially on guard for in the next months?

How can we, as a group, help with a certain problem?

You can certainly make up your own question if you prefer, but remember that it needs to apply to everyone present, and it should not be for a selfish purpose.]

READER: [Shuffle and cut the deck according to your usual practice. You will then lay out a single card toward the center of the table. This is the main issue facing the group. You should interpret it according to your own deck. Pass the deck *clockwise* to the person on your left, who cuts the deck, draws a single card, and lays it faceup in front of them. Interpret it according to your deck. When you have finished, the person passes the deck to their left, and the next person does the same thing. This proceeds until the deck has come all the way around. Cut the deck and draw a card for yourself. If you see connections, it is appropriate to discuss all the cards together or the relation of certain cards to the group card in the center. This is very individual and can be as long or as short as the reading suggests. If the group members like, they may do another round with another question, beginning with someone asking it and you shuffling. This may proceed several times but should not exceed four or five because the amount of energy involved is certain to tire you and diminish the quality of the answers. When the last reading has been completed, put the deck away.]

WARDEN: Mighty Ones, we thank you for this good counsel. May we use the guidance you have given us well, and in all things act for the benefit of all, not for merely our own. We take your counsel in that spirit. Thank you. [Take the sword or knife and begin walking *counterclockwise* around the circle. Visualize retracing the line of protection, erasing it as you go. When you return to your starting point, sheathe the blade and extinguish the white candle.]

NORTHERN QUARTER/READER: Uriel, Angel of Winter and Night, thank you for your protection. [Extinguish green candle.]

WESTERN QUARTER: Gabriel, Angel of Autumn and Evening, thank you for your protection. [Extinguish blue candle.]

SOUTHERN QUARTER/WARDEN: Michael, Angel of Summer and of Day, thank you for your protection. [Extinguish red candle.]

EASTERN QUARTER: Raphael, Angel of Spring and of Morning, thank you for your protection. [Extinguish yellow candle.]

WARDEN: Thank you all. The circle is open.

Afterward you may wish to eat a meal together to ground everyone and to take time to talk about the reading. This may be a potluck, something more elaborate, or you can just order a pizza. The important thing is that people have a chance to talk and to ground the energy of the experience. Some things to consider in addition to discussing the questions and answers you received:

- What did you think of the style of the ritual? How is it the same or different from what you are used to?
- How does it feel to balance energy this way? Is this something that you would like to incorporate more often, or is it not comfortable for you?
- What do you think of doing something in the form of nearly a hundred years ago, before the Pagan revival? Does it speak to you or not?
- How does this style relate to the season it was current in, the previous saecular Winter?

Once you have had time to talk and ground, the ritual is concluded.

If you are solitary and are not able to do the ritual because it inherently calls for at least two people, consider the following questions after reading the ritual's instructions:

- What did you think of the style of the ritual? How is it the same or different from what you expected?
- Is this a ritual you would feel comfortable doing? Why or why not?
- What do you think of doing something in the form of nearly a hundred years ago, before the Pagan revival? Does it speak to you or not?
- How does this style relate to the season it was current in, the previous saecular Winter?
- If you were able to re-create this ritual, what part would you take? What questions would you ask?

You may wish to write the answers to these questions in a journal if you are keeping one as you work through this book.

Drawing Conclusions

As we look back on the season of Winter in the last saeculum, 1925–1945, one thing that must strike us is how great the difference is between the beginning and end of that period. This is roughly analogous to the period 2005–2025. In other words, we can expect 2025 to be as different from 2005 as 1945 was from 1925. It's a lot of motion. We are going through major changes as a society and as individuals. No wonder our world seems so out of control sometimes!

However, now that we've found our charts—the navigational data left by previous generations—we're ready for the next step of determining our own voyage on the sea of Winter. In order to reach a goal, the first thing you need is to know where you're starting from. In the next chapter, we'll examine where we were at the beginning of our current Winter.

..... **Chapter 5** .....

Where Were You
When Winter Began?

Sometime around 2005, Winter began. Future historians will debate exactly when it happened. Was it on September 11, with the attacks in New York, in Washington, and on Flight 93? Was it in March 2003 when we began the war in Iraq? Was it in September 2008 with the stock market crash, the beginning of the largest economic disruption since the Great Depression? Was it with the election of Barack Obama eight weeks later? Just as we can debate what moment in the 1920s began the last Winter, a hundred years from now people will parse out our newscasts and our cultural artifacts trying to decide what point in the mid-2000s was unmistakably Winter. From this short distance it's hard to know what the key moment was, but it really doesn't matter. We know that Winter began.

Who were you, personally? What were you doing? We're going to find our bearings in this current Winter by taking a little trip back to 2000, just before our current Winter began. Year 2000 was Samhain on the Great Wheel of the Saeculum, when we entered the dark of the year.

Samhain

First of all, 2000 is not the present. Just as there were massive cultural changes between 1920 and 1940, so there are massive cultural changes between 2000 and 2020. Let's look at the cultural changes first. In 2000

- there were no smartphones—they hadn't been invented yet;
- Bill Clinton was president of the United States;
- there was no Facebook;
- there was no Twitter;
- same-sex marriage was not legal anywhere—in thirteen states it was still illegal to have sex with a consenting adult of the same sex;
- top movies included *X-Men*, *The Perfect Storm*, *Gladiator*, and *Crouching Tiger, Hidden Dragon*;
- the hot new TV shows included *CSI*, *Malcolm in the Middle*, *Dora the Explorer*, and *Survivor*;
- Destiny's Child rocked it with "Say My Name," Faith Hill sang "Breathe," and Santana was "Smooth"; and
- the United States was not at war with anybody.

Year 2000 is a moment in the past. In 2000, the generational constellation was different than in 2020.

The Greatest Generation was still with us in large numbers, the youngest of them 75 years old. Many were still active in their communities and as voters. While their influence was waning, they were not yet gone. In fact, Senator Strom Thurmond, the president pro tempore of the Senate, belonged to the Lost Generation. The Supreme Court was dominated by the Greatest Generation, including Chief Justice Rehnquist.

The Silent Generation, ages 57–74, held most of the institutional power in the United States as elected officials, CEOs, owners and operators, tenured professors, and so on. Their emphasis on bipartisanship, cooperation, and compromise frustrated their Baby Boomer juniors.

The Baby Boomers, ages 40–56, had ignited the Culture Wars and were fighting them bitterly. They were just beginning to finally escape from cautious elders, ushering in a new era of scorched-earth politics rather than emphasizing incremental change. Left and right prepared for the fight to come.

Generation X, ages 19–39, had just completely come of age and occupied the junior positions in work and community. Now becoming parents and workers themselves, they were largely focused on personal things rather than the state of the world, though their polarization was inevitable in the partisan atmosphere of the Culture Wars.

The Millennials, ages 18 and younger, were the teens and children. They were the ones who had the most to lose from instability, and many parents protected them a great deal, giving rise to the term "helicopter parent."

Journaling Exercise

If you have journals, datebooks and calendars, photographs, or other memoirs from 2000, get them out and look through them. Take some time doing this. Really remember who you were and what you were doing.

If you are too young to have your own memoirs of 2000, look back at pictures or documents that others may have saved for you. Maybe it's your kindergarten picture and the artwork you did, or even your discharge papers from the hospital where you were born. Ask yourself the following questions:

- What did you think and feel? Was this a good time or bad time? Would you return there if you could?

- What changes would you potentially make if you could talk to your 2000 self? What would you never want to change?

- How is your life different now than it was in 2000? Do you live somewhere different? Work somewhere different? Have different people in your life?

When you have finished thinking about your personal experience, consider these questions as well:

- How is the world better than it was in 2000? How is it worse?

- What trends today were apparent in 2000 but not important or not really in the mainstream?

- How have technologies that didn't exist in 2000 impacted your life? How are those impacts positive and how are they negative?

Once you have recorded your thoughts, move on to the next section.

Winter Comes

It's tempting to think that if we could go back, Winter could have been prevented. What if Al Gore had become president in 2001? What if there had been no Iraq War? What if, somehow, September 11 had never happened?

It's important to remember that Winter is a natural part of the turning seasons of the saeculum. Specific events may or may not happen, just as the weather on a particular day in January may vary, but Winter as a season is inevitable.

Why does Winter come? According to the sociologists William Strauss and Neil Howe, Winter comes when the generational cycle reaches a certain point—when what they call Idealist Generations like the Baby Boomers gain institutional control and power. The deep and painful rifts in that generation were manifest in 1970, but because of Greatest Generation and Silent Generation control of institutions and of the power positions in government, finance, industry, and media, these conflicts were tempered.[36] Through the seventies, eighties, and into the nineties, slow and deliberate elders pushed compromise and bipartisanship to left and right alike, whether they sought to stymie the Democratic "Watergate Babies" or Newt Gingrich's "Republican Revolution." Eventually, they weren't there anymore. To better understand what happened, let's tell a story.

Bob and Frank

Once upon a time, in about 1965, there were two brothers named Bob and Frank. They grew up in a clean, neat suburb in a little brick house with three

---

36. William Strauss and Neil Howe, *The Fourth Turning* (New York: Broadway Books, 1997).

bedrooms: one for Mom and Dad, one for Bob, and one for Frank. Both boys were smart and made good grades and both were good at sports. They were inseparable, best buddies, blood brothers.

Bob got into a good state university. There, he started thinking about some things. He decided that the war in Vietnam was wrong and that Martin Luther King Jr. was a hero and that his parents sat in their comfortable living room listening to Walter Cronkite and didn't really care about the rest of the world.

Frank got into a good state university. There, he started thinking about some things. People said that it was wrong that he admired his father who had served in the Pacific in World War II and that he was a square for not smoking pot and joining protests.

Bob and Frank both got draft notices, and they both did some thinking. Bob married his girlfriend, Sandra. They were already living together and married men were usually deferred. He and Sandra moved into an apartment near the university.

Frank reported when he was called and dropped out of school. He was sent to basic training, and in 1970 he was sent to Vietnam. He saw terrible things. He did terrible things. Terrible things happened to him. He came home. He moved back into his room in the little brick house.

Bob and Sandra had a baby girl, Allison. Fathers were deferred. Bob started graduate school. Sandra worked full-time while he was in school, and Bob watched Sesame Street with Allison.

Frank married his girlfriend, Debbie. They had a baby girl named Karen. Frank worked as a mechanic at the truck stop out by the interstate. He drank a lot and dreamed about getting on a motorcycle and just leaving. One day he did. When he got back, Debbie said that she wanted a divorce. She got one, and she kept Karen.

There was Christmas with Mom and Dad in 1976. Dad and Bob had a big fight because Bob had grown long hair. Dad said Bob was a hippie fool. Bob said Dad was a bigoted Archie Bunker. Frank told Bob not to talk to their father that way because it was disrespectful. Bob said Frank was a baby killer and asked him how many children he'd killed. Allison started crying. Frank said that if Bob wasn't his brother he'd take a swing at him. Mom asked everyone to calm down. Sandra said they were leaving, and they did.

They didn't come back for six years. Frank took care of Dad when he had his heart attack. Frank married a woman named Bev, and Karen stayed with him some. They bought a house, and eventually part interest in a garage.

Bob and Sandra moved to a Sunbelt city and bought a beautiful house in a gated community. Allison went to a top-ranked university and studied abroad. Bob voted for Bill Clinton.

Frank voted for Bob Dole. He went to AA and got sober and became a Sunday school teacher. He took care of Bev's two little boys because their dad had no contact. Karen went to community college and became an RN.

Bob voted for John Kerry. He valued expertise and globalism and he thought the Iraq War was a travesty. Frank voted for George W. Bush. He wished he was young enough to go after Bin Laden.

Dad died in 2005. Mom died a few months later. Bob and Frank had a huge fight at the house right after the funeral. They screamed at each other while Allison and Karen stood on the porch looking helpless, Allison in her tailored black pantsuit and Karen in her black dress. Bob and Frank haven't spoken since.

In 2016 Bob volunteered for Hillary Clinton. In 2016 Frank voted for Donald Trump.

I'm not sure if it was Karen or Allison who said to the other on Facebook, "Do we have to be enemies?" Whoever it was, the other one didn't answer. But she didn't block her either.

———— • ————

This is how we got here. Our bitter internal wars aren't wars between different tribes. They're literally brother against brother. The bottom line is that Bob and Frank, in all their manifestations in society, want to punish each other. They want to hurt each other. They want to avenge a lifetime of injuries. Can Bob and Frank be reconciled? Can Allison and Karen find common ground, or do they have to simply fight their fathers' wars?

History suggests that Bob and Frank won't reconcile. Osiris and Set, Abel and Cain—the oldest stories tell us that this will end when one of them is dead. This is the furnace that fuels the crisis, the war between brothers, mythic in its scope and as personal as Bob and Frank. This is what makes Winter come. The brothers each call their army to them and they fight until one or the other is annihilated. They use their power as older men, as leaders in society, to clash with one another. It's not actually about others at all, any more than Set and Osiris is about the government of Egypt or Cain and Abel is about proper ways to worship. It's about punishing the one you know best. It's fratricide.

Can that clash be prevented? Probably not. Can its outcome be altered? Assuredly. How the crisis ends rests with Allison and Karen. They are the ones who decide what happens ultimately and how the winners and losers treat one another and the larger society. The people who decide what happens going forward, after Bob and Frank, are Allison and Karen.

Bob and Frank are a microcosm for what we call the Culture Wars. Let's explore that concept in more depth.

The Culture Wars

Winter began for me late in 2005. I got a fundraising email for an LGBT+ organization I had worked for the previous year. It wasn't the usual polite request for money to fund programs. It was a long screed about how there were Catholic secret societies that had private assassins and were attempting to undermine pro-gay court rulings, and that to fight the Catholic secret societies I should immediately send money. I simply boggled. Then I thought, some intern in Development has lost their mind. I forwarded the email to a very senior person at the organization I had worked with, asking if he'd seen it and saying that this was not at all the tenor I expected from the organization. He replied saying something like, "Yeah, but the numbers are looking really good on this one. High open rate, high response rate." I replied again and said, "But it's not true. This is BS. This is ripped out of the *Da Vinci Code*! This is a fictional bunch of secret assassins in a book. We've got plenty to fundraise on with the Federal Marriage Amendment, which is real legislation in Congress, and Rick Santorum in the Senate who wants to run for president. Those are real problems." He replied, "Yeah, but it's performing really well."

Let me be clear: frightening people with lies so they will give you money is morally wrong. Doing so in a bigoted way and using lies to turn people against a religious, ethnic, racial, or sexual minority is evil.

This is when Winter came for me: when I saw my side, my former coworkers—people I liked, even my friends—justifying evil in the name of winning.

This was the Culture War. It was the historical moment when the polarization of the Baby Boomer generation split society and erased gray areas. Let's pit LGBT+ people against Catholics and that's okay. Then is it okay to pit straight people against Pagans? Or rural people against Jews?

There had always been people on the fringe who believed that the government had put chips in their brain or that a cabal of Jewish bankers was ruling the world or that Satanists were infiltrating preschools to steal babies for human sacrifice, but until this time, responsible people didn't buy into these conspiracies, and ultimately they would stop them. This is how we navigated the eighties and nineties, and as someone twice wary, both queer and Pagan, the saving grace was that when some nut would get off on "witches want to steal your children" or "gays want to spread AIDS because they serve the devil," sensible people would call BS. Now the reasonable people, even people who ought to know better because they were also part of a marginalized group, thought this behavior was okay if it made a lot of money for their cause.

In the late 2000s we moved into the war of all against all just as we had in the 1930s. Every group was constantly exhorted to anger against every other group. Every misunderstanding became oppression. Every difference of opinion was unsolvable. The old methods—following rules of order, polite discourse, and even the assumption of innocence—were thrown out by people drunk on outrage. It happened in knitting groups, fan communities, parent klatches, and many other places where previously people with differing opinions and differing identities met and mingled. Groups tore themselves apart. Mostly, everyone lost. Fifteen years later, what seems most to remain is sadness among those who lost the joy in participating in things they loved, who lost friends, and who lost community. Winter's storms blew away support networks first.

Social media didn't cause this. This impulse was here before the rise of Facebook and Twitter. But social media made it possible for the storm to go global in the same way that the rise of radio made it possible for demagogues to address millions instead of hundreds in the last Winter. In the 1930s, ideas that previously would have been limited in scope because a speaker simply couldn't have reached a national audience could suddenly reach millions instantly—and daily. When we listen to recordings of American anti-Semites like Charles Coughlin, they're not saying anything new. The slurs they repeated had been around for decades. What was new was that Charles Coughlin could tell millions of people directly, in their own living rooms, that Jewish bankers were behind the stock market crash and the Great Depression.[37] At its peak, his radio show had nearly twenty million listeners each day. His newsletter, *Social Justice*, reprinted the anti-Semitic *Protocols of the Elders of Zion*, a fraudulent document supposedly belonging to a secret Jewish conspiracy to rule the world that in fact had been manufactured by Russian intelligence.[38]

Is this beginning to sound familiar? A new technology suddenly means that conspiracy theorists run wild, reaching a new, wide audience, while in the background Russian intelligence is laughing? We have been in this season before. Our grandparents or our great-grandparents listened to Coughlin, turned off the radio, or railed against him. They wondered who to trust. They wondered what information was real. They wondered who their enemies were, because one thing every speaker on every side hammered home was this—they are coming for you. Be afraid. And donate by return post.

We, with the benefit of eighty years distance, can say that Hitler was a real threat and so was Stalin. They did sign a pact on August 23, 1939, which directly led to the invasion of Poland on September 1, 1939. We can parse out which voices were homegrown Fascists and which were funded directly by Hitler's SS, as many "grassroots organizations" in the late 1930s were.[39]

---

37. Sheldon Marcus, *Father Coughlin* (Boston: Little Brown and Company, 1972).

38. Charles Tull, *Father Coughlin and the New Deal* (New York: Syracuse University Press, 1965).

39. Steven J. Ross, *Hitler in Los Angeles* (New York: Bloomsbury, 2017).

This was true on the left as well as on the right. For example, one of the bestselling anti-Fascist books was *J'Accuse!: The Men Who Betrayed France*, by a freedom fighter named André Simon. A veteran of the Spanish Civil War, Simon held high-profile Hollywood fundraisers, suave in his bespoke tuxedo, a great Resistance hero. The only problem was that there was no such person as André Simon, and he'd never been anywhere near the Spanish Civil War. He was Czech, a Russian secret agent named Otto Katz who reported directly to the GRU.[40]

Historians, with the benefit of hindsight and access to millions of documents, can trace propaganda and separate it from activism, can determine the difference between real atrocities and fake news. Those who lived at the time could not do this, any more than you can tell if something you see on Facebook is a real grassroots thing or comes from a Russian bot.

Like those who came before us, when we don't know who is telling us the truth or whether those we trust are manipulating that trust, we must be guided by our hearts. We must look at everything through the lens of our values and weigh them against the principles that guide our lives.

Values

We have a tendency to think of "values voters" as people on the right, as conservative Christians who aren't very tolerant of others. So what are we? Voters without values? People who just do whatever suits them?

Of course not. As individuals and as a community, we have strong values: values that may set us apart from the mainstream, values that are very important to us and inform how we live our lives. It's time to reclaim the word "values." Having values doesn't mean being conservative or reactionary, and saying that some things aren't okay isn't being intolerant. While there are many different paths within the Pagan community, there are some values that nearly everyone can agree on. Let's explore some examples of those Pagan values and consider how they can be our strengths in this current Winter.

---

40. Jonathan Miles, *The Dangerous Otto Katz* (New York: Bloomsbury, 2010).

We will consider four values—hospitality, honor, plurality, and reverence for the earth—as beginning points for identifying what Pagan values mean to us.

Hospitality

Many ancient religions stressed the importance of hospitality. From the beliefs of the Old North to the religions of the Mediterranean, from Africa to the New World and beyond, hospitality was an important virtue attested to in story after story. Many cultures had a story like this: a god or goddess is traveling the world in disguise and comes to the home of some poor but good people. These people invite the traveler in, not realizing they are hosting divinity. They give them the best bed to sleep in and the best food to eat, humble as they may be. They share all that they have. Touched by their virtue, the god reveals themself and blesses the poor family, telling them that they will prosper from this day forward as a result of their kindness.

These stories embody a powerful truth: we never know who is asking for our help, and we must always do our utmost to help the stranger among us. Parsimony and selfishness are for the unworthy. The worthy give freely. The old stories have ugly words for the selfish: meager, skinflint, churlish. Saying "I got mine" and refusing to share is being a small person. Meanwhile, those who give magnanimously are favored by the gods.

As you work through the chapters on Winter to come, think about how we, as Pagans, can embody the virtue of hospitality. How can we, as parts of the greater community, live our values?

Honor

Honor is old-fashioned, as old-fashioned as old gods. Honor is doing what's hard because you promised. It's keeping your word even when it's inconvenient. It's fighting fair even when your opponent doesn't. It's protecting the weak and using your strength to guard, not to intimidate. Honor is doing your duty. It's not descending to an enemy's level. It's fair competition and good sportsmanship. It's loyalty to those who depend on you. It is believing, as my father said, that "other people's bad behavior doesn't excuse yours," whether the others behaving badly are your enemies or your friends.

We believe in honor. We believe in heroism.

Yes, that's old-fashioned. And those are values worth believing in, values that are worth living by. Long before there was philosophy there was honor. The old stories are hero stories—stories about men and women who behaved in accordance with honor, even when that meant terrible sacrifices. Who are the villains in so many old tales? Those who behaved without honor, who lied and stole, who killed the helpless and offended gods and humans with their crimes. Heroes don't do those things.

Today, we need honor. We need its companions, dignity and honesty and duty. We can choose to be honest. We can choose to be dignified in our own interactions with others. We can choose to do our duty in our own lives. As we continue deeper into Winter, consider how this value—honor—is part of our response to crisis, both as individuals and as a community.

Plurality

This is something that is inherent in polytheism: There is no one right way. There is no single answer. Life is not a multiple-choice question with three wrong answers and one correct, the way that many of us are taught from early childhood. There are lots of different ways of living just as there are lots of different ways of worshiping, and all of them are correct. If one person worships Cerridwen and another Shakti, if one worships Horus and another Mercury, all of them are right.

We are not a tapestry woven into a single beautiful and elaborate pattern, but a patchwork quilt. Some of the pieces are different sizes, some are colors that don't go together, some are intricately embroidered and some are embarrassingly plain, but the whole effect is stunning. It's gorgeous. It's almost incomprehensibly large. And it's never completely finished. We don't want each piece to conform. We like it the way it is.

Because we live in a complex society, we have much to teach the greater society about how to comprehend plurality. Rather than engaging in a tug-of-war about whose answer is correct, we can say that it's okay for different people to have different correct answers. It's even okay for different communities to reach different consensuses and to live according to the principles they've consented to, just as we know that different spiritual communities choose to govern themselves differently, teach differently, and live differently. The key is consent—people can choose how their community will live, and those who do not agree with the conclusion reached by the majority in that community have the freedom to leave and live somewhere more in concert with their beliefs. We understand that for anyone, no matter how well-meaning, to impose beliefs on others without their consent is wrong.

As we move through this season and the chapters that follow, consider how the Pagan value of understanding and valuing plurality comes into play.

The World Is Our Home

Earth is not a room we're passing through on the way to someplace better. This is our home. Whether we embrace reincarnation as part of our belief systems or not, we are of the earth. It's not "fallen." It's not a place we've been sent to because we're deprived of Paradise. This is our home.

For many of us who believe that we have lived and will live again, the future of Earth is our own future. If we make a mess for a hundred years from now, we will be here living in the mess. It's not about our children, or at least not only about them—it's about our own personal futures as well. Taking care of the earth, being responsible and helping to solve this environmental crisis, is not an act of altruism. It's an act of self-interest. We are going to live with the outcomes of our actions. If we make our world uninhabitable, we will be the ones living with the consequences.

More than that, we value the world and all that's in it. It's not a temptation. It's a treasure. The sensual feeling of sand under our feet, the wind against our skin, the warmth of sunshine after days of cold, the heady scent of ripe summer vegetables—these are good. These are gifts. Our religion teaches us to value them and to value the experiences of the body. We are not meant for suffering. We are meant for joy. The world is meant to be a place of beauty and wonder, and when it is not, it needs to be restored to wholeness just as we do when we are suffering. We love the world.

As we experience the season of Winter, think about how our love for the world and the natural cycles of life helps us to live in this season.

Journaling Exercise

You will need your journal for this (or a computer or an alternate means of journaling as you prefer). Consider the following questions about the values suggested above:

- How do you respond to hospitality as a value? Is this something that has meaning in your life? How do you feel that you live out this value? Are there ways in which you would like to be more hospitable?

- How do you respond to honor as a value? Are there things about it that make you uncomfortable? How do you feel about duty, dignity, honesty, and self-sacrifice? How do you think your community responds to those ideas?

- How do you feel about plurality? What are some ways that you are different from those you are close to? How do you honor those differences? Do you feel pressure to conform to some community ideal? Are there things that you believe that you would not be comfortable saying publicly because you think they would be disapproved of?

- How do you relate to the earth? Where do you most appreciate earth's gifts? How do you help with this current environmental crisis in ways great or small? How is winter a part of a natural cycle?

- What other ideas would you classify as Pagan values? What do you think is most important to you? What Pagan values would you like to see more widely embraced?

Let's not be afraid of using the word "values." Let's not be afraid of claiming our beliefs. We have much to offer the greater community in this time of crisis. Our values can help guide not just ourselves but those around us as we navigate this season.

We've looked at where we are—Winter began, and this is who we are and what our present position is. Now we can begin to chart our course through this season of crisis based on the maps we've inherited and our current knowledge. Let's move forward into the season of Winter together.

····· Chapter 6 ·····

The Gathering Storm

The first part of Winter is the gathering storm, when it begins to become clear that an era of crisis is coming. At first, most people deny the signs of winter. It's just a chilly day. It's just a little bad weather. But eventually, the signs that nature gives us are unmistakable—the leaves have fallen from the trees, the nights are long and the dark gathers round, and even the days are no longer warm and pleasant. We must accept that winter is upon us and plan accordingly. Remember, the only way to spring from Samhain is through winter. The wheel does not turn backward.

As the storms gather, problems may begin to seem insurmountable. Rather than pretending that Winter isn't really here or denying that the problems exist, people become hopeless. How can anyone get through this? How can we live in a time that is so barren, so dark?

Of course we can live through it, as generation after generation has before us. We can get through Winter the same way our ancestors did: with planning, community, and faith. The time will come when we must live day-to-day as the storm rages around us; however, before the storm breaks, we must do our best to plan for the challenges ahead. The following three chapters will help us prepare before the storm breaks.

The first calls upon Athena Strategos to help us prepare physically—on a mundane as well as a spiritual level—for what lies ahead. The second removes the barriers that discord creates in our lives that prevent us from taking constructive action. The third calls upon Hermes to help us prepare mentally by cutting out the cluttered communications in our lives and leaving clear channels open so that we are aware, informed, kind, and cautious while both receiving and giving correct information. Remember, we cannot make good decisions about the events to come if we don't both realistically understand our own situation with its vulnerabilities and strengths and receive truthful information about events as they happen.

Now, at this point I am making assumptions about you. I am presuming that you want to preserve democratic institutions. I'm presuming that you don't want a humanitarian crisis and floods of American refugees. I'm presuming that you want a future built on citizens who consent to fair laws rather than a dictatorship, a theocracy, or a corporate oligarchy. I'm not assuming that you don't want systemic change, or that you don't identify major issues in the United States today that need to be reformed, or that you necessarily want the product of the Crisis era to produce a single unified nation where the United States is today—just that you want changes, whether large or small, to take place without incredible bloodshed and destruction. I'm also assuming that you personally wish to survive the crisis, and that you want your friends and loved ones to do so as well. This is the framework for the strategic planning that follows. These rituals and meditations are intended to move toward these goals. If these are not your goals, these rituals are not for you.

Athena Strategos—Strategic Planning

Athena Strategos is the aspect of the goddess Athena who is the companion of heroes. She is the goddess who whispers in Odysseus's ear, advising him on his battles in the Trojan War and in his long wanderings.

Athena is a warrior goddess, but she is also the goddess of wisdom. She is not the patron of the scream-and-leap type of hero. She prefers calm, sensible, wily, and clever champions, those who make a great plan and carry it through. In the *Iliad*, she is the patron of Odysseus, who comes up with a way to take the impenetrable city of Troy through a ruse. In the story, the Greeks have besieged the city for years without being able to capture it and things have reached a stalemate. Athena counsels Odysseus to use his head rather than his strength, and he comes up with the plan for the Trojan horse. The Greeks build a big wooden horse and then leave it before the gates of Troy as they apparently give up and sail away, while actually just going around the headland a few miles. Hidden in the horse are Odysseus and a few men. They wait. Thinking that the Greeks have given up, the Trojans celebrate and bring the horse into the city as a symbol of victory. Later, in the wee hours of the morning after everyone has gone to bed, Odysseus and his men sneak out of the horse and open the gates of the city to let in the Greek army. The city falls in flames, the Greeks finally winning. Thus, Athena is the goddess of strategy. It's not just about fighting—it's about fighting smarter.

In historic times, Athena was the patron of the Athenian navy, the advisor of those who protected fragile democracy. She was likewise the patron of the Delian League, a NATO-like association of city-states that joined together to fight against the Persian Empire's expansion in the Aegean. It is completely appropriate to invoke her assistance to make good plans for the future, and to ask for her help in preserving democratic institutions.

Asking the Help of Athena Strategos

There are three main steps in this rite in making strategic plans: identifying the potential problems, identifying resources, and creating a plan to use those resources to address the problems. It is tempting to skip one or both of the first steps, but doing so will leave out important things that contribute to the last step. In the planning phase, while there is still time, it's critical to think through all the steps. You may do all the steps at the same time, or you may split up this rite as appropriate. The first part is a journaling exercise that consists of asking Athena to help you think strategically.

You will need:

a light blue candle (it does not matter what size)

an image of an owl (This could be a small statuette, a postcard, or a picture printed off the internet. Owls are Athena's animal; they belong to Athena, and therefore symbolize her wisdom and counsel.)

writing materials (a notebook, a journal, or a computer if you prefer to record your thoughts that way)

Optional extras:
Incense, preferably myrrh, and a burner

Assemble these items before you in a quiet place and light the candle and/or incense. Say, "Athena Strategos, companion of heroes, please help me to plan for the coming season of crisis so that I may act wisely, kindly, bravely, and in a timely fashion."

Now comes the hard part. With clear eyes and logical thought, write down the potential problems that you can identify relating to where you live. For example, climate change is causing many different weather-related issues and can be anticipated to cause many more in the next ten years. However, which conditions are likely to affect you depends on where you live. If you live in Northern California, you are extremely unlikely to experience a hurricane, but wildfires are almost certain to be a concern. Conversely, if you live in Miami or Savannah or Houston, it is quite likely that you will experience a hurricane and much less likely a wildfire. If you live in Nebraska, neither are likely, but tornado season is growing increasingly lengthy and perilous. Identify the climate-change-related challenges that are most likely where you live.

Next, consider the political situation. While new problems seem to erupt almost daily in the news, it is possible to imagine a number of different scenarios that lead to major civil disruption. Consider the following questions.

Where do you live?

- Do you live near centers of national political importance, such as Washington DC or New York? (Control of these centers is critical, making them targets for any disruption.)
- Do you live near locations of military importance, near major bases like Norfolk or San Diego, or near nuclear missile silos or command centers? (Again, control of these centers is critical.)
- Do you live near locations of strategic importance—major oil and gas pipelines, refineries and storage facilities, major shipping ports, crossings

on our northern and southern borders, major dams or nuclear power plants? Do you live near bridges or mountain passes that are choke points for transportation? (Because control of these locations is important, they are the most likely to be fought over by any actors involved.)

- How dependent is your community on climate control to preserve livable conditions? (For example, if you live in Minnesota and there is no electrical power for an extended period in the winter, people will die from the cold. If you live in Phoenix and there is no electrical power for an extended period in the summer, people will die from the heat. People cannot survive temperatures below zero or above 100°F without some means of heating and cooling.)

What do you depend on?

- How far away is your electrical power generator? How dependent is your community on power lines bringing in electricity from more than fifty miles away?

- How much of your food is grown locally as compared to shipped a long distance? (Many places have some food grown locally, but consider if that was everything that everyone in your community could access for several weeks. How soon would there be a humanitarian crisis? For example, after Superstorm Sandy, an infrastructure study by the city of New York determined that the city has a four- to five-day supply of food within the five boroughs. Any longer disruption would mean that food would become unavailable. It would functionally become unavailable to many people sooner because the food is not evenly distributed at all locations, but clustered around certain hubs.)[41]

- How much of your community's infrastructure is dependent on oil and gas brought in from a long distance? How would a gasoline shortage impact your community? (If, for example, you have buses that run on natural

---

41. "Five Borough Food Flow: 2016 New York City Food Distribution and Resiliency Study Results," New York City Economic Development Corporation and the Mayor's Office of Recovery and Resiliency, 2016, https://www1.nyc.gov/assets/foodpolicy/downloads/pdf/2016_food_supply_resiliency_study_results.pdf.

gas that is produced reasonably locally, you will be less dependent on pipelines that run thousands of miles.)

- Do you need medications that might be in short supply in the event of a civil disruption?
- Are you responsible for vulnerable people—children, people with disabilities, elderly people—who would need help in the event of a crisis? Are you, yourself, vulnerable?

Where is your money?

- Are you financially dependent on checks that may be disrupted by governmental problems or extended shutdowns? For example, do you receive Social Security or federal retirement, or are you an active-duty military or federal employee?
- Do you have your money or retirement savings in the stock market? Are you prepared for a disruption of the stock market or a major loss in value?

These and other questions are not easy to think about, but you must think about them in a logical and clear-eyed way in order to prepare for the challenges ahead.

Once you have identified the major risk factors in your personal situation, move on to the next part. Do not leave the exercise at this point.

Consider the image of the owl and focus your thoughts. You are going to ask Athena to help you formulate answers to the problems you have identified.

Say, "Athena Strategos, help me to plan wisely and well, so that I and those I love may weather this storm as best we can. Help me to find the best-case scenarios."

There are best-case scenarios. Even if you are an elderly person on Social Security who lives in the Washington DC metro area in a low-lying house in the flood plain near major air bases and in an area that is essentially inaccessible except by bridges and are dependent on power and food traveling hundreds of miles, there is still a best-case scenario. There are still the best possible outcomes for you.

First, if you have many risk factors that are related to where you live, consider what you can change and what you can't. Remember, all these preparations need to be completed by late 2020 to early 2021, so ameliorations which involve changing jobs or moving may not be possible. But they may be. If you are living in a very vulnerable area and you are able to move elsewhere, it is certainly worth considering. You will not be able to change many of the risk factors if you stay. For example, a community may be accessible only by going through a choke point. In the recent California wildfires, one key vulnerability was that in some locations there was a single road leading in and out of the community. As all the residents tried to evacuate at once, that road became gridlocked and impassable. As Houston Mayor Sylvester Turner said about not ordering a mandatory evacuation of the city as Hurricane Harvey approached, "You literally cannot put 6.5 million people on the road."[42] At a certain point, the infrastructure is incapable of handling the evacuation.

On a smaller scale, it may be possible to improve things by relocation within the same community. For example, if you live in a community prone to wildfires or vulnerable to hurricanes, there are safer and less safe parts of the area. You are more likely to flood if you are on low ground near water than if you are on high ground. Even if you remain in the same community, you may be able to move to a different dwelling in a safer location. Likewise, some of the strategic targets in an armed conflict are specific places like airports, power plants, and oil and gas storage facilities. If you live next to the airport, you are more likely to be involved than if you live across town.

If you are able to change your dwelling even within the same general area in order to minimize these risks, you should consider it. However, moving may not be an option, or you may already be in a fairly low-risk location. In that case, your preparation may revolve around more typical disaster planning—having adequate supplies of medication, water, nonperishable food, emergency radios, and so on. There are many fine lists of disaster supplies

---

42. Camila Domonoske, "Why Didn't Officials Order the Evacuation of Houston?" NPR, August 28, 2017, https://www.npr.org/sections/thetwo-way/2017/08/28/546721363/why-didn-t-officials-order-the-evacuation-of-houston.

maintained by the Red Cross, emergency management agencies, and various nonprofits, so it's not necessary to go into all of that here.

For example, the Red Cross website offers disaster planning guidelines beginning with identifying the most likely natural disasters where you live and working through to the recommended supplies to put in your emergency kit. Ready.gov, a website maintained by FEMA, also has excellent examples of building emergency supplies as well as evacuation instructions. The National Hurricane Center has a great compilation of links for everything hurricane-related, though many also pertain to other disasters. In terms of emergency supplies, many retailers offer preprepared kits as well as solar-powered chargers for electronic devices, dehydrated foods that require little preparation, crank-powered radios, and other supplies. Many of these things are useful to have under normal circumstances to deal with severe weather, whether winter or tropical storms, and can be kept for an extended period of time if they are not needed right away.

Let's simply add a few things that point to a broader crisis than a weather event that affects only a part of the country:

- Paper road maps: If the Global Positioning System satellites were damaged or inaccessible, it would be months if not years before they were replaced. If you had no GPS for months, you would need paper maps.

- Alternate means of communicating with friends and family members if you could not use major social networks or the internet in general: From physical destruction of servers to seizure of these assets, control of communications is a strategic imperative in war. You need a way to reach people that doesn't depend on these assets.

- Access to funds that are kept locally: In this age of national banking, many people have their money or their mortgages or their retirement funds in institutions that are thousands of miles away from where they live. If your money were suddenly in a different country or on the other side of a war zone, what would happen? Would you be able to get to your money, use your accounts, and bank normally? If possible, consider moving your money into a local credit union that is managed within the same state where you live.

Check in with yourself. At this point in your strategic planning session, you may be feeling overwhelmed, frightened, or that this is too much. "This is crazy prepper stuff! Nothing is going to happen! Everything is going to be okay. There can't be a war here. There can't be some big disaster. This is nutty."

As nutty as things that have already happened in the last few years?

Not all of these things will happen. But some will. We cannot know which ones—war, civil unrest, natural disaster—but we know that in the season of Winter, there will be storms. Last Winter we had World War II. The Winter before that we had the Civil War. The Winter before that we had the American Revolution. In each of those times, people hoped and prayed and believed that nothing would happen right up until the moment it did.

But some got ahead of the curve. Some protected their own treasures, the people they loved, their life's work, so that they and the things they cared about survived. Some took the steps beforehand so that they were ready to participate in the crisis to the best of their ability, to bring these crises to the best resolution they could. That's you. That's your job right now. If you prepare for a hurricane and you're lucky—it hits another city instead of yours—you were fortunate this time, but it's certainly not nutty to prepare. It's wise.

We are now ready for the end of the rite, this journaling exercise in which you have asked the goddess to help you plan. When you have reached a point in your planning where you feel comfortable and in control, thank Athena Strategos. Say, "Lady of Owls, Preserver of Democracy, Companion of Heroes, thank you for being my companion. Help me to be clear-eyed and worthy of Your regard." Blow out the candle and extinguish the incense if you have used it. You may wish to light it again as you continue your preparations and call on Athena Strategos again for her assistance.

In the next chapter we will work on removing the barriers that discord creates in our lives that prevent us from taking the constructive actions we have planned.

····· Chapter 7 ·····

Clearing Discord

The city is burning. Flames rise above the fine walls, blackening with soot the stones that archaeologists will one day identify as Troy VI. Well-dried cedar and cypress beams burn like torches. The cloud of black smoke can be seen for miles out to sea, a choking plume like a sacrificial altar, reeking of flesh and precious woods. When the wind turns, the smoke washes over the crowds on the beach by the lower city.

The Greeks are casting lots for the women and children, deciding who will be whose slave. Some of the women say nothing, standing almost in a stupor, their clothes ripped and bloodied. Some cling to children or to one another. Others scream as Andromache did when her infant son was torn from her arms and thrown from the walls. Still others curse ineffectually, but a blow to the side of the head from the pommel of a sword will shut them up, possibly forever.

The war is over. The Trojan heroes are dead; Hector's dead body dragged behind a chariot is torn to pieces, rendering him unrecognizable pulp. They are dead. There is no one to save anybody.

And yet the Greeks do not celebrate. They separate the slaves grimly, apparently oblivious to children crying as they are separated from their mothers. They are the winners, and yet Achilles is dead, and Patroclus, and Palamedes, and Ajax. Agamemnon the High King lives under a terrible curse, as do many of the survivors who will return home to find murder in their own houses. They have won. They hold the burning city. But they will get no joy from it, no strength, no profit. Even Menelaus, who has now retrieved his unfaithful wife, Helen, has what? A wife who ran away from him and is brought back by force of arms? He sought her in love and keeps her in hatred. There will be no peace in the houses of any of the victors. The Trojan War is over.

———— • ————

The *Iliad*[43] tells us the story of the Trojan War and the gods and men who fought in it. The *Odyssey*[44] and many other works, like the *Oresteia*,[45] tell us of the terrible fates of the Greeks who conquered Troy. They were, for the ancient Greeks and Romans, the ultimate story of war. Its pointless suffering was the subject of many surviving works of art, including Euripides's *The Trojan Women* and *Hecuba*.[46] But why did all these terrible events take place?

According to the myth, it was because of the goddess Eris, known to the Romans as Discordia. In the ancient stories, Discordia is a goddess who loves strife. Hers is not the competition and war of Mars or Ares nor the strategic brilliance of Athena or Minerva, but simply strife. Discordia is pain for pain's sake—the pointless destruction of people or things just to watch them burn, the tearing down of people or places not so new things can grow, but simply because it's pleasurable to set people against each other and watch them hurt. In the story of the Trojan War, all of this terrible strife—the dead children, the rapes, the killings, the burning of the city—is because Eris offered an apple to the goddess who was most beautiful and set Paris to judge the winner. The pointless contest, and the strife that emerged from it, destroyed not only Troy but almost everyone who participated in these events on either side. No one, innocent or guilty, could escape. Discordia collapsed a civilization.

---

43. Homer, *The Iliad* (New York: Penguin Classics, 1998).

44. Homer, *The Odyssey* (New York: Penguin Classics, 1999).

45. Aeschylus, *The Oresteia,* trans. Hugh Lloyd-Jones (New York: Bloomsbury, 2014).

46. Euripides, *The Trojan Women and Other Plays*, trans. James Morwood (Oxford: Oxford University Press, 2000).

And she enjoyed it. The other gods and goddesses wanted their side to win, to protect their beloved worshipers, to see justice done or to avenge someone fallen. Discordia just wanted the lulz. She wanted what Thomas Hobbes called "the war of all against all."

This is not a concept of Discordia that can be used for productive ends. This is not the radical breakdown of unnecessary institutions or unfair laws, but the complete destruction of civilization. This concept of discord is no one's friend. She is no one's patron and no one is her beloved. She is on nobody's side. She just wants to hurt *everyone*.

Today, this version of discord is rampant in our civilization. Her effects are everywhere. This is the mentality of finding videos of mass shootings funny. This is the mentality of laughing at weeping family members. This is the mentality of posting pictures of the bodies of the victims with funny captions, of livestreaming murder, of abusing animals on camera. This is not about breaking taboos. This is about enjoying people's pain and hurting people and animals for amusement.

Discordia doesn't have a political party or a side. She just wants everyone to fight. She's opportunistic. Whoever gives her the greatest scope to hurt people is a temporary tool. She will seduce and incite anyone, twist even good intentions to evil ends. Just as in the story of the Trojan War, the goal is for the heroes to annihilate each other.

Why should we limit Discordia? Because unbound discord will destroy us. If we treat those around us with anger and fear, if we let wrath and terror rule our relationships, we will shortly find ourselves without relationships. If we act intemperately and fearfully in our professional lives, we will diminish our capacity to work by losing jobs and gaining a bad reputation. If we, as a society, become incapable of cooperation and trust, we become incapable of being a society—of working together to provide even the most basic functions of an organized community.

The ancients recognized this. Having had historical periods of extreme unrest, of revolution, of mob rule, of purges and upheavals that threatened the lives, property, and safety of every person in their society, they understood that there had to be civic rites to restore normalcy. While great civic rites may be beyond the scope of what you can do, each person can take steps to limit Discordia's power in their own lives.

Here are two rites to do that, each of which should be followed by the rite to invoke Hermes to restore clear communications.

Banishing Discordia I: Closing the Conduit

You can't empty a bathtub with the water running. Even if you open the drain, the bathtub will continue to fill. At best, the water coming in will flow back out and you will maintain the same water level, but usually the water will keep rising. If you want to empty the bathtub, first you have to turn off the water. For many of us, the conduit by which Discordia enters our lives is our online interactions.

First, you must want to close the conduit. If you really want to spend your time arguing with Russian bots on the internet, or you enjoy the rush of power from putting down another person or ganging up on someone who "deserves it," this will not work for you. You have to intentionally choose to limit Discordia's power and to walk away from the thrill of her service.

And it is thrilling. The lure of revenge, the pleasure of righteous anger, the rush of hurting someone you can't see when hitting feels like justice— those are very rewarding feelings. It is a kind of joy to be an avenging angel, a Fury incarnate. However, unbound by justice and reason, untempered by compassion, this is simply discord.

To continue with this rite, consider whether you are willing to step away from that rush. Are you willing to be bound by justice and compassion? Are you willing to limit your actions with reason and kindness? If not, then this is not for you. If so, move to step two.

Identify Discordia's Offering

Second, identify the offering that you are making that feeds Discordia. For many of us, those who do not work in politics or advocacy, our main point of conflict is through social media. That is where we are eating a constant diet of anger and pain—a daily dose of outrage, outrageous behavior, cruelty, intolerance, and things that make us fearful. For most of us, there isn't a mob outside our door or people walking into our places of employment to scream death threats at us. Most of us do not have friends who regularly berate us or hurt us. Yet we do online. We have "friends" who say terrible things. We encounter strangers who tell us we're awful people. We are parts of communities that spread hopelessness and anger.

That doesn't mean that all communities are this way, or that all outrage is toxic. However, here are some questions to ask yourself when considering if a community or platform is creating discord.

- How do I feel when I've been on this platform? Do I feel empowered or fearful? Do I feel encouraged or hopeless? Do I feel positively about the people I'm interacting with, or angry and upset?

- How do the people here treat one another? If these interactions were in person, would you feel they were appropriate? (E.g., fifty people ganging up on a teenager for misspeaking—would you feel comfortable watching fifty adults surround a sixteen-year-old to scream at her in a parking lot?)

- Over time, is this community lifting each other up or putting each other down? Is success congratulated or treated jealously? Are the leaders supportive of others, or do they use their power to brag or to reduce others?

- Are there a few people who are always causing problems? Are there strangers who pass through spreading trouble? If so, the community may be a target of deliberate bad actors, whether politically or personally motivated.

- Does this community generalize and focus anger at specific groups of people based on their ethnic, religious, racial, or other characteristics rather than on individual actions or policies?

Not every online interaction is toxic, and not every community spreads discord, though some notoriously do. When you have identified the avenue by which Discordia is coming into your life, move on to the next step.

The Rite

You will need:

a black candle and something to light it

your computer, phone, tablet, or device with which you usually access that
platform

Light the black candle. Open the platform and hold in your mind the discord you see as you speak.

Say, "Discordia, I do not want you in my life. I will feed the Furies no more. I will give you no more offerings."

Then delete your account.

You will feel pushback. You are probably feeling it right now.

"I can't do that. I need it. I have to have it for work. I have friends who are there. I need it. I need it. I don't have to delete my account. I could bargain. I could just be on less. I could limit my time instead of going cold turkey."

That is Discordia sucking you back in. That is the maelstrom trying to pull you back into the swirling waters full of dangerous beasts. You must have resolve. You must be certain of your intention.

It's hard. This is the hero's battle—Horus in the underworld bearing a light on a boat over fearful waters. You will feel a struggle. You will hesitate, not certain whether to click or not, arguing with yourself.

"I have to have it for work."

If you truly have to have a professional account on whatever platform, then have one that has no content except your professional content. But if it is truly a professional account, then you probably have not identified it as a source of discord. A LinkedIn account full of former coworkers is not the pipe that is filling the bathtub.

"I'll miss everyone here."

There are other platforms and other ways to reach people. If they truly matter to you, you do not need this particular piece of software to keep in touch.

Push through it. Imagine yourself turning off the water. Delete the account. With each step of the process, imagine the water slowing, first from a rush to a stream, then from a stream to a trickle.

And then it's done. Close your browser or app and breathe in the candle-light.

Say, "Discordia, I abjure you."

You may feel empty, as though a presence has departed, as though a huge noise that has been constant in the background has suddenly silenced. Those voices are stilled. The shouting mob that has been a click away is gone. They're not outside your door anymore. The howling voices of Discordia's winds are gone.

Put out the candle you've used. You will not use it again. Take it outside and bury it or throw it in a public trash can away from where you live.

Banishing Discordia II: Creating a Compact

Discord is chaos: the absence of restraint, order, and even common sense. The opposite of discord is not conformity. The opposite of chaos is just rules. One way to banish Discordia from one's online life is to create rules that preserve justice, compassion, and privacy, and prevent harassment, bullying, and negativity. Ideally, each platform's Terms of Service would ensure that users' privacy was protected and that they were not dogpiled, harassed, or subjected to endless streams of abuse and negativity. Unfortunately, as we know, this is not the case. If you must use one of the platforms notorious for these kinds of problems, what can you do?

First, make sure that your privacy settings are as robust as possible, opting out of every possible intrusion. Second, use control settings to mute or silence discussions that are not profitable, opt out of seeing content that you do not wish to see, and unfriend people who are constant sources of drama and pain. Then create a compact—your own Terms of Service, the rules by which you will conduct yourself online.

The Rite

You will need:

a black candle and something to light it

paper

a pen or pencil

Light your black candle. As you do, state your intention clearly and say, "I will not contribute to discord." You are going to put away this chaos and regain control of your experience, and by doing so make the online world a better place, not only for you, but for everyone with whom you come in contact.

Take the writing instrument and paper—you are going to write your compact in longhand, and then you are going to keep it where you can see it when you are online. Think about what you wish the Terms of Service were. Think about what rules you wish the platforms you use required people to follow. Think about what you respect and don't respect in others' behavior. Some examples of statements are the following:

- I will not post pictures of anyone without their permission unless they are readily available to the public (e.g., an artist's publicity photos), and I will not provide identifying information or personal information for anyone, even if I am angry with them or don't like them.

- I will not use profanity or swear at anyone, nor will I use demeaning or insulting language about anybody.

- This is my professional account, so I will behave at all times as though my clients, bosses, or employees were reading it. I will behave as though I were in a physical workplace, not a social space.

- I will not post, reblog, like, or otherwise distribute information that I do not know is true. I will not spread gossip, allegations, rumors, information that can't be corroborated, or what may be falsehoods, lies, or fake news.

- I will only distribute information that I personally know is true (e.g., the video taken out my window) or that comes from reputable news sources.

- I will not participate in shaming anyone. I will especially not participate in shaming people who are very young, have disabilities, or are economically disadvantaged, or for other reasons I feel strongly about.

- If I see harassment, bullying, dogpiling, or online abuse, I will immediately report it. I will report it even if my friends are doing it. I will report it even if the person being harassed is a member of a group I do not like. If I am a moderator, or if the abuse takes place in a space I have responsibility for, I will exert my maximum effort to remove the harasser.

- I will hold community leaders to the same high standards in virtual spaces as in real spaces. If it would be inappropriate to say or do in person, it is inappropriate to say or do it online. I will not follow leaders who do not set a worthy example.

Other statements may certainly be created as you see fit, as long as they contribute to rational, kind discourse.

When you have reached the end of your statements, add "I do so swear," and sign it with your full legal name. You are signing a contract, a compact. You are making a sacred oath. Feel the weight of it. Now say aloud, "Discordia, I abjure you."

You may feel frightened or you may feel free. You may find this intense. Put the paper where you will see it and be reminded of what you have sworn.

Once you have cleared the largest source of discord in your life, you are ready to fill that space with things that contribute to positive action. Remember, the goal is to prepare for the crisis so that you and your loved ones will survive and contribute to building a better world. Once you have limited the fear and anger that paralyze people and prevent constructive action, you are ready to begin that constructive action. It's time to move on to the next part.

Invoking Hermes

One of the most critical issues that has emerged as we face this Crisis era is the issue of clear and truthful communications. The internet has provided many opportunities for both good and ill, linking people with the like-minded, facilitating communications between people who would otherwise never meet, tying far-flung families and friends together. It has also allowed radical or disgruntled people who would have otherwise been isolated to organize into hate groups, proliferated bullying of anyone who dissents from a community viewpoint, and allowed falsehoods spread as fact to compete with actual news. Diplomacy is conducted in 280 characters, heads of state threaten war or civil insurrection on social media, and literally millions see false information deceptively spread by foreign governments. As individuals, how do we know what to trust? How do we deal with being dogpiled, swatted, or doxxed, or the threat of these things? How do we deal with the constant negativity that many of us face online? How do we tell the difference between what is genuine activism on behalf of a cause we support and deliberate manipulation by a foreign government that means to divide us and create hatred between groups?

Hermes rules communication and media and should be invoked to bring clarity and truth in messages. The purpose of this rite is to turn negative interactions into positive ones and falsehood into truth. Some of this takes place in sacred space, which involves stating your intentions. However, intentions without follow-through are just words. The last steps of this ritual —actually making the second and third offerings you plan—must be done outside of sacred space in the days to come.

The Rite

You will need:

a gold or yellow candle

incense, preferably frankincense, and a burner

something to light the candle and incense with

your computer or phone or whatever you use to access the internet

Light the gold or yellow candle and a fresh stick or cone of incense. Take a few moments to breathe deep and center.

Hold in your mind the image of Hermes, running fleet-footed to deliver messages accurately and truthfully. You are going to make an offering to him instead, a gift that gives both to him and to its human recipients.

"Hermes, god of Communication and Media, of clear and truthful news and information, of messages used for positive means, help me to use media to bring light and happiness rather than pain and suffering. May my offerings be to your honor."

The First Offering

Consider someone you admire. Perhaps it's an author or an actor or an artist whose work you have always enjoyed, or perhaps it's a public figure of a different kind, or even a local business you have had great experiences with—but it should be someone you do not know personally. Now give them something right now. You are sitting at your computer. Maybe it's an amazing review on Yelp or Amazon, or a fantastic testimonial on Etsy or Goodreads. It should be all positive. It should not equivocate or criticize. This is an offering, a gift of the best. Tell someone you don't know how much you have appreciated their work.

As you do, you may feel a sense of satisfaction. You may feel happy. Imagine how pleased this person will be when they read your words! Imagine their pleasure and joy. Imagine that you are making their day, and that even though you will not see their happiness, you are giving happiness to someone who has given happiness to you.

Say, "Hermes, I give this in your honor."

The Second Offering

Consider someone you know casually who has helped you or who has brought you pleasure. Maybe it's the pharmacist who straightened out your prescription, or the bus driver who waited for you when it was raining. Maybe it's a local restaurant that you love to go to because they're always so friendly. Maybe it's someone at work who made your life easier, or the honest mechanic who told you that you didn't need an $800 part.

If you are able to right now, thank them. Send them an email. Post a review publicly praising them. Say, "Hermes, I give this in your honor."

Plan what you are going to do if it is something you are not able to do right now, such as leaving them a generous tip the next time you see them, or talking to their boss and telling them how fantastic they are. Imagine the positive consequences of your action. Imagine their unexpected joy. Imagine how the review may help them, how the tip will allow them to do something they need or want to do, how the word to their boss may improve their lives. Imagine the trail of happiness you are creating.

Say, "Hermes, I swear to do this in your honor." While you can't do it this moment in sacred space, you are vowing to do so in the next few days. Make sure that you follow through on your promise to the god.

The Third Offering

Consider someone you know well and care about. Perhaps this is a dear friend or a family member. Perhaps it's a parent or a child, a spouse or partner, or a new friend you have just welcomed into your life. Think of something you particularly love about them.

If you want to email them or call them right now, in sacred space, you can do so. Tell them that they're awesome and why you think so. Tell them that you're glad they're in your life. Tell them how much you love the thing you identified—they're kind, insightful, funny, charming, generous, brave, strong. Revel in their pleasure at being complimented.

If you are not able to tell them right now how much you appreciate them, say, "Hermes, I will do this in your honor." Plan how you will do it and do it in the next few days. Make sure that you keep your promise to the god.

When you have either completed your offerings or have planned how you will do so, say, "Hermes, thank you for helping me communicate positively and truthfully." Put out the candle and incense.

Making a Habit of Offering to Hermes

Many of us spend a certain amount of time a day on social media. Now that we've turned off the water flowing in that spreads discord, we may find ourselves with twitching fingers. We have a habit. We want to go back on whatever it is and "just see." We miss it. We have the time that we daily made an offering to Discordia, and now that time is empty.

Fill it with offerings to Hermes instead. Go somewhere else and leave an offering. Join a different community that has a more positive nature. Leave reviews on artwork that you like. Make supportive comments to people who are struggling. Donate to fundraisers for people in need, even if your gift is small. Give something daily, even if it's just a kind word, in the space where you would have liked or retweeted or reposted anger. Be the light you wish to encounter. It can be just as addictive and fulfilling as serving Discordia. Do it intentionally. Say to yourself, aloud if you are able to, "Hermes, I dedicate this good to you."

The Storm Rages

····· Chapter 8 ·····

Preserving the Seed

Twenty-Five Hundred Years Ago

It is a beautiful summer morning, and a procession winds its way through the streets of the town from the open gates to the temple. It's still a small building: four columns across the front, one large room inside with a second behind to store equipment for various rites. The procession is joyful, young and old, men and women alike, many of them bringing offerings. Most commonly these are bread shaped into long breadsticks like snakes, some of them ornamented with seed eyes. Others bring clay snakes, elaborate and painted, while others simply roll clay out by hand, the way children do it.

At the front of the procession, a big black ox pulls a cart decorated with stalks of wheat. In the cart are eight large clay pots, unpainted and undecorated except for symbols painted across the top: the names of the farmers this grain belongs to. The grains come from the threshing floor, and this is the last of this summer's crop—the seed grain that must be conserved and not baked, for it will be planted in the spring to sprout as next year's crop. It's important that this happens and that the seed remains undisturbed until March. If it's eaten or used profligately, if not enough is saved, or if it is spoiled or lost to rot or rodents, the entire community will go hungry next year.

The cart stops before the temple, and men hurry forward to unload each of the big pots. As each is brought under the portico of the temple, it is blessed by a priestess, an older woman with graying hair who wears a wreath of pomegranate twigs bound together with white wool yarn. She is the chief priestess, her husband the chief priest, and this rite is hers, for she reigns over the land beneath where the grain must go. After each pot is blessed, it's moved with some great effort inside the temple. Today a trapdoor has been opened in the floor of the temple, a short flight of stairs leading down beneath the building. There are ample lamps beneath, and the men haul the pots down to join twenty or so others arranged in neat ranks. The chamber is snug and dry; the stone foundations and floor are neatly joined, and the stones and temple above protect it completely. Each pot is labeled, each put in its proper place.

When the last pot has been put beneath, the offerings come. In twos and threes people descend into the *mundus cereris*, the chamber beneath, leaving their snakes and bread. It's a mystery rite, but it also serves a practical purpose: everyone in the community knows that the grain is safely stored and everyone knows that their chief wealth is appropriately labeled and honestly sealed. The mundus cereris is a vault, not simply in the holy sense, but also in the sense of a bank vault.

When the last offerings have been put below, the priestess speaks a prayer for the safety of the grain, leaving it in the protection of the *di inferi*, the gods beneath, Pater Dis and Queen Proserpina. Then the mundus is sealed, the cover stone replaced over the chamber beneath. It will only be opened twice before spring, both on days sacred to the gods beneath: on October 5, when Ceres herself is honored; and November 8, when Proserpina descends to the underworld to reign there during the winter. In the safest place in the community, the seeds of the community's future harvests will be kept until once again spring comes and it is time to plant them.[47]

---

47. W. Warde Fowler, *The Religious Experience of the Roman People* (London: Macmillan and Co., 1911).

Conserving the Seed

Today, as we look forward to an unpredictable and perhaps harsh Winter, we must consider the seed we wish to conserve for Spring. Simply put, what harvests of this saeculum do we wish to carry over into the new saeculum? As we pay so much attention to what will be lost or destroyed and whether that destruction is timely or tragic, we must also focus on what we wish to preserve. If we put nothing in the mundus cereris, if we place no seed off limits for protection, we will have no seed in the Spring. As a community, we must decide what things of worth we wish to keep. As individuals, we each can decide what goes in our pot—what share of the harvest is our personal contribution to next Spring's sowing.

Let's begin by considering the achievements of this saeculum. What things of lasting value have happened in the United States since 1945? What advances have been made? What contributions have been made to humanity? What do we like? What do we value about our culture and our time? These advancements can be legal, cultural, scientific, and so on. Here are a few examples to begin thinking about.

Prior to the introduction of the polio vaccine in 1953, thousands of people, many of them children, contracted polio each year. In the United States in 1952, more than three thousand people died and more than fifty-seven thousand contracted polio, many of them living with severe disabilities afterward. However, the introduction and widespread adoption of the vaccine reduced polio cases in the United States to zero by the year 2000.[48] Nobody died. Nobody became disabled. The polio vaccine, and other vaccines like it, is something we wish to keep in the next saeculum.

The Civil Rights Act of 1964 outlawed discrimination on the basis of race, sex, religion, or national origin. It was a landmark law, reaching deep into society and serving as the basis to give greater equality to millions of people—whether they were previously prevented from applying for certain jobs because they were female, denied housing because they were African-American, or not

---

48. Sophie Ochmann and Max Roser, "Polio," OurWorldinData.org, November 9, 2017, https://ourworldindata.org/polio.

hired because they were Jews, to give a few examples. The breadth of the impact of this law is incredible. While it did not, of course, solve all problems overnight, it provided a solid legal basis for fighting for equality and remedying injustice. The Civil Rights Act of 1964 is something we'd like to put in the mundus cereris to preserve for the next generations.

We also may wish to preserve cultural treasures. Perhaps we hope that fifty years from now people will still be moved by the words of a certain author or may still draw inspiration from the Star Trek or Marvel universes. Perhaps certain musicians' work is a cultural treasure, whether that's *Cabaret* or *Hamilton*, the Rolling Stones or Beyoncé. Perhaps you can't imagine a world without Steven Spielberg's movies or Suzanne Collins's Hunger Games. What are the cultural treasures created in the United States since 1945 that you wish to keep to inspire, inflame, comfort, and instruct future generations?

Maybe what we'd like to preserve are institutions. For example, in 2018 about sixty-three million Americans received Social Security benefits. Of those, forty-six million were elderly people who depended on these benefits to pay their bills and live day-to-day. Another eleven million were disabled people who were not able to work. Lastly, six million were children who had lost one or both parents and relied on Social Security benefits to survive.[49] If those checks stopped coming, millions of vulnerable people would be plunged into abject poverty. We would face a humanitarian disaster of our own making on a scale never before experienced. Perhaps Social Security is something we'd like to put in the mundus cereris.

Maybe we'd also like to preserve ideas or beliefs. For example, the religious ideals of Neopaganism have developed and changed since 1945, spiritual traditions evolving with new generations of practitioners. Maybe we think that's valuable and we'd like to keep it.

Perhaps we'd like to keep other ideas—e.g., the idea that same-sex relationships aren't unhealthy and that same-sex attraction isn't a mental illness. That happened in 1987—homosexuality was removed from the *Diagnostic and Statistical Manual of Mental Disorders* as a mental illness, though some

---

49. "Fact Sheet," Social Security Administration, retrieved December 22, 2018, https://www.ssa .gov/news/press/factsheets/colafacts2018.pdf.

therapists and psychologists continued to practice as though it were for decades after. The change from classification as a mental disorder to modern affirmative psychotherapy and the social change this supported completely transformed the lives of LGBT+ Americans.[50]

These are simply some examples of things we might wish to preserve and carry forward into the next saeculum, things we wish to prevent from being destroyed in the fire of ekpyrosis. There are many others as well, and no two people's lists will be the same.

As you consider what you wish to preserve, begin making a list. You can simply jot down your thoughts, or you can carefully put them into categories and elaborate on each. The more effort and intention you put into your list, the more effective the next rite will be.

As you do this, you may think of things in your personal life that you want to preserve, such as the lives of loved ones, a career that is important to you, or relationships in your community that matter to you. If you wish, you may add them to your list. However, please remember that the point of the rite is the good of the community. Many of us are not used to thinking like leaders and planning for the good of the community rather than just ourselves. It's fine to add a few things that are important to you personally but not really to the big picture; however, keep your focus on society, not on your personal hopes. For example, I may want to preserve my own friendships within the LGBT+ community, but that is a much smaller and less important goal than preserving the freedoms LGBT+ people have achieved since the 1960s! In this rite, we are thinking about the big picture as we prepare for our role as leaders in the Crisis era.

Into the Mundus Cereris

Few of us have access to a temple, and many of us also have no basements or crawl spaces beneath our homes where we can store something on a long-term

---

50. Neel Burton MD, "When Homosexuality Stopped Being a Mental Disorder," *Psychology Today*, September 18, 2015, https://www.psychologytoday.com/us/blog/hide-and-seek/201509/when-homosexuality-stopped-being-mental-disorder.

basis; however, we can capture the symbolism of the ancient rites of the mundus cereris in ways that still speak to us today.

You will need:

a clean jar or pot with a lid

a permanent marker that can write on glass or ceramics (like Sharpie oil-based markers)

paper, pen, and scissors

a black candle

modeling clay, child's play clay (like Play-Doh), potter's clay, polymer clay (like Sculpey), or small plastic toy snakes

your list of things you wish to preserve

a glass of red wine or pomegranate juice

a small bowl

a pomegranate

images of Proserpina and Father Dis (whether these are effigies or printed photographs of paintings, drawings, or ancient statues. If you are artistic, you can make your own.)

The purpose of this rite is to preserve those things that we wish to carry over into the next saeculum. These are the ideas, cultural treasures, laws, institutions, and ways of living that you hope are still here in 2027, and that you, personally, will help preserve.

To do so, we are going to make a jar of our seeds to store through the Winter. How long will that be? We don't know, no more than the ancients knew when winter would end. But, like them, we can guess an approximate date. You will probably store this seed until 2025–2027.

The Rite

Sit down with the images of Father Dis and Proserpina visible and all your other supplies at hand.

Light the black candle. Say, "Father Dis, Proserpina, please attend to my words. Please accept my offering."

Cut the pomegranate in half and place it before the images. Take the red wine or pomegranate juice and pour some into a small bowl in libation. Take time to hold their images in your mind. Visualize them listening to you, Father Dis bearded, solemn, and concerned, a cornucopia at his feet from which spill gems and golden coins—all the hidden treasures of the dark places, riches unimaginable. Beside him sits Proserpina, her golden hair braided tight beneath a winter crown of twigs and berries, unmelting frost glistening on them like silver. She listens, her eyes kind, to your words.

Say, "Winter has come, and we must conserve that which is dear to us until Spring comes again. Secret ones, lord and lady of the world below, help us to preserve these precious seeds until the world warms again."

Carefully, and with thought for each, write the things you wish to conserve on the paper, saying each one out loud as you do so. Focus on the social good each one produces. You may add a few that are purely personal; however, keep the focus on the big picture. Then cut the paper so that each item is on its own small slip of paper. Once again, name each one as you fold it in half and put it in the jar.

"Please protect these precious things," you say. "May these snakes symbolize your protection." Use the clay or modeling clay to make snakes just as small children do, rolling them out against a table or surface. If you are so inclined, you can add eyes or other markings to them, making them appear more finished and lifelike. When you have completed a few snakes, put them in the pot or jar with the slips of paper. (If you prefer to fire your snakes or paint them, you can make your snakes ahead of time and simply put them in the jar at this point in the rite. Your snakes may be as elaborate or as simple as you like.) If you are not able to make your own snakes, you may use plastic toy snakes instead.

Visualize Father Dis and Proserpina watching. He is nodding, glad to be asked to take on his traditional task. She is concerned but hopeful, looking forward to the day this jar will be opened.

Put the lid on the jar or pot. Say, "Secret ones who rule below, these seeds were stored by *your name*. Please preserve them for me, or for those I love or who need them in Spring." Write your name on the container with the marker.

If you are able to put the jar into a basement or crawl space, do so. Carry it to the appropriate place with due ceremony and put it where it will not be disturbed. If you do not have a basement or crawl space, place the jar somewhere low and dark where it will not be bothered. The back corner of a kitchen cabinet is a possibility, or the drawer beneath the stove. Under a bathroom sink is another possibility. This place is your symbolic foundation, your symbolic storehouse.

If you have placed it in a crawl space with a dirt floor or under a sink, pour the wine you have poured in libation near where you "buried" the jar. If not, take the wine outside and pour it on the earth or into a potted plant.

Eat one of the pomegranate seeds, savoring its taste. Say, "Thank you, Proserpina. Thank you, Father Dis." Blow out the candle.

You may use the rest of the pomegranate and wine as you wish, though consuming them with friends or loved ones is especially appropriate.

This rite may also be modified if you are undergoing a personal Winter—a fallow time or crisis in your life—and may focus on purely personal things you wish to preserve.

In the days, weeks, months, and years to come, leave the jar alone. Do not open it. Do not retrieve it. Leave it safe in the world below, safe in the hands of Father Dis and Proserpina. No matter how much you are tempted to get it out, don't. Wait until Spring. One day, Spring will come.

····· **Chapter 9** ·····

Havens in the Storm

As Hurricane Florence bore down on the coasts of North and South Carolina, tens of thousands of people fled vulnerable coastal areas. However, for many the cost of evacuation is prohibitive and the logistics difficult. Can I take my dog? Can I afford two, six, fourteen nights in a hotel? While emergency management and public shelters help many, a new and extremely positive use for social media has arisen that is helping more and more people with each disaster. In the last few years, various media platforms have hosted initiatives by private individuals to help those fleeing storms, wildfires, and even volcanic eruptions. As Florence approached, families and individuals in western North Carolina and Tennessee invited total strangers to seek refuge with them. As one woman in Tennessee said of the twenty-six people her family hosted during Hurricane Irma, "My sister came up from Florida first, then our really good friends who are originally from Venezuela, and we put them up. And then we started getting phone call after phone call from friends and friends of friends that had nowhere to go. One guy came in crying at four in the morning because he had a two–year-old and a very pregnant wife. They were so relieved to be able to finally put their head down in a safe place."[51]

---

51. Gianluca Mezzofiore, "These People Are Opening Their Homes to Hurricane Florence Evacuees," CNN, September 11, 2018, https://www.cnn.com/2018/09/11/us/evacuees-hurricane-florence-shelter-trnd/index.html.

Many people who became hosts had themselves fled hurricanes in the past and understood what the evacuees were going through.

This movement toward people helping others individually rather than as an organized group has also been important in situations of civil disturbance. For example, #RoomforManchester was the tag used by people in the United Kingdom to help those who were unable to get home because of the terrorist bombing at the Ariana Grande concert.[52] As various bombings and civil disturbances have occurred, people in Europe and the United States have invited stranded strangers to stay.

This is not a new idea. In the last Crisis era during World War II, more than two million vulnerable children had to be evacuated from London and Southern England because of air raids. People all across the country and in Canada opened their homes for years at a time to these children who needed to be sent out of urban areas for their safety. Tens of thousands of families and individuals welcomed these children, these internal refugees.[53] Could we do the same?

Of course we could. And we are likely to need to. Whatever shape the crisis takes—whether war, civil disturbance, natural disaster, or some combination—people will flee. They will try to evacuate if they can. They will try to get their children out. They will try to get their elderly parents out. And they will go—in cars with their dogs and cats, in planes that take off overloaded, or on their own feet like the last evacuees in the recent California wildfires. They will go to wherever offers a safe haven.

Will you be that haven? If you, yourself, do not live in an area of immediate danger, can you open your home to others? Can you plan ahead to be a place of refuge? Even if you feel that you do not have "critical skills" for

52. Helena Horton, "#RoomForManchester: Kind Strangers Open Up Their Homes to Those Affected by Manchester Arena Attack," *The Telegraph*, May 23, 2017, https://www.telegraph .co.uk/news/2017/05/23/offers-help-pour-social-media-following-manchester-arena -incident/.

53. Julie Summers, "Children of the Wartime Evacuation," *The Guardian*, March 11, 2011, https://www.theguardian.com/lifeandstyle/2011/mar/12/children-evacuation-london -second-world-war.

the coming crisis, creating a haven is something you can do that will be vital, whether you are able to help one person or twenty-six.

Inventorying Your Strengths

The following questions will help you identify your strengths: the things that you already have that contribute to being a haven.

Do you have a guest room? A finished basement? A pull-out sofa that someone could stay on overnight if they were stuck in a city center? Do you have the physical space to host one or more people for one or more days?

What is that space like? How many people can stay there? How long could they stay there? One night? A few days? A few weeks? Longer?

Is the space suitable for pets? Children? Elderly people or those with limited mobility? For example, if you have a fenced yard and a dog, would you welcome someone evacuating with dogs? Is the room a basement family room that is accessible only by steep stairs and is unsuitable for someone with mobility issues?

Is there a way for a person or people to eat? Use the bathroom? Shower?

Do you have skills that would let you assist someone who needed extra help in some way? Experience with the elderly? With disabilities? With children? If, for example, you run a home daycare or have a toddler of your own, could you help a young mother evacuating with a baby? If your home is already childproofed and you have baby gear, you are already there.

Who would you find easy to host? Who would you find too much? Be honest in this assessment. If you have a pull-out couch in a small apartment, you probably mean one or two people for a very short time. If you have an unoccupied mother-in-law suite, you could take many more for a longer period.

Once you have considered your strengths, consider next the character of your haven and the work you wish it to do.

Inside the Haven

Hero stories are full of havens: enchanted castles, hidden valleys, schools for unusual children, secret caves, and more. Havens are the place where heroes break their journeys, are protected in childhood, seek wisdom and guidance, and recover from their physical, mental, and spiritual injuries. Every haven is different, and even within the same story havens may have different purposes. For example, in *The Lord of the Rings*, Frodo and the Fellowship are restored in two very different havens: Rivendell and Lorien. Rivendell is a place of learning and wise counsel with a magnificent library and a diverse collection of good-hearted people visiting from all over their world. Lorien is almost otherworldly, a spiritual place that seems remote and pristine amid a darkening world and where guidance takes the form of riddles and visions. Rivendell is led by Master Elrond, whose learning and hospitality make his house a home for many travelers. Lorien is ruled by Galadriel and Celeborn, who keep the borders of this hidden land despite great risk while it appears to be untouched and untouchable. Yet both are havens, and both are places where the heroes find rest and replenishment.

Consider these and other fictional havens: Which would you like to live in? Which would you like to rule? Xavier's School for Gifted Youngsters or Miss Peregrine's Home for Peculiar Children? Rivendell? Lorien? Avalon? Helen Magnus's Sanctuary?

What would you like your haven to feel like? What would you like people to think when they walk through the door? What values do you want it to support? Learning? Peace? Action? Is it a library? An armory? A temple? A home? Is it hidden to all but a select few? Open to any wanderers in need?

Imagine your ideal haven. Maybe it's a Victorian house with many rooms full of kind monsters. Maybe it's a cave hidden high in the mountains with a secret door. Perhaps it's a lodge overlooking a remote valley where animals mingle with human visitors. Maybe it's a city brownstone that looks like any other until you discover the secret door to the sublevels. Be creative. Imagine your ideal and walk through it in your mind.

What does a visitor see when they arrive? Where do they sleep? What do they eat? Are there special features—a room with floor-to-ceiling bookshelves, an archery range, a waterfall?

What does it smell like? Does it smell like delicious home cooking or like a deep pine forest? Like faint, complex perfume or the sawdust of the workshop?

What does the visitor hear? Faraway flutes? Thumping bass? Running water?

Visualize your ideal haven as completely as you can. Then name it. What is this secret place?

Once you've visualized and named your haven, it's time to consider how your actual physical haven can be more like your ideal. For this part you may need to work together if you have a shared space with a partner, friend, or other family members and incorporate different ideas of what a haven could be. This step may also seem difficult. For example, if your ideal haven is a remote mountain lodge beneath great fir trees and you actually live in a small city apartment, the gulf between ideal and reality may seem huge. However, even if the disparity is great, you can still work toward making your space feel like your ideal, even if it's as simple a change as a coat of paint.

One way to identify how to make the physical haven more like the ideal is to make a word cloud. On a blank piece of paper, jot down the attributes that come to mind when you think of your ideal. For example, "cozy," "library," "comfortable," "ancient," "quiet," "peaceful," "autumn," and "wood" might compose a word cloud. How can you make your space feel more like a peaceful, cozy, ancient library? Don't just think about obvious things like paint or furniture, but also about scent and touch. For example, there are many home scents that remind people of autumn that could make your space feel more like your word cloud.

As you consider the feel of your haven, also consider the practical logistics of someone staying with you. Are there changes you could make that would make it easier and more pleasant for someone to stay, or that would let you accommodate different people? For example, a pack-n-play crib costs less than $50, lets you safely host a young child, and folds up easily to fit in a closet or under a bed. Do those basement steps need repair or a new handrail? Would putting a small refrigerator and a microwave in that basement bedroom turn it into a suite? In a city apartment, a pull-out couch instead of a conventional one would make room for one or two people to sleep.

Also consider things that would make your haven more comfortable for the people who live there all the time. A new light to make the steps to the basement easier to see? A rug on that chilly floor? Fixing the tile in the bathroom that almost nobody ever uses?

Once you have decided upon the feel of your haven and the steps you plan to take to make your physical space more like your ideal, it's time to dedicate your haven.

Dedicating the Haven

First, you need a name. The Murphy's Cave. Pinewoods. The Lair. Imladris. Jared and Anna's Castle. The Green Box. Avalon. Halloween House. It can be formal or silly, descriptive or classic. What matters is that the name fits your ideal.

Second, consider which deity or deities you wish to invoke to protect your home. If you have a patron deity, they are an obvious choice. If not, consider protective deities of hearth and home in a tradition you are comfortable in. For example, Brigid is a good choice if you work in a Celtic tradition, or Bes or Bastet in an Egyptian. If you are not certain or if you prefer a classical tradition, you can use the dedication that follows to invoke Vesta, the Roman goddess of hearth and home.

The main thing most people remember about Vesta is that in Rome she was served by virgin priestesses, but Vesta herself was not described as a young girl. Vesta is usually pictured as a "matron," meaning a married woman in her thirties or forties, the mistress of a household and the woman responsible for its smooth operation. A matron, therefore, is in the position of domestic responsibility, and is therefore a suitable face for the goddess who protects and preserves the home.

A Rite to Ask Vesta to Hallow the Home

Now we are prepared to actually do the rite to invite Vesta to hallow our homes.

You will need:

a candle (preferably an LED candle so that you may leave it lit and unattended) a place to put the candle (preferably in the kitchen. A shelf, a windowsill, or a space on the countertop will all do perfectly.)

some kind of sign with the name of your haven (It can be a wooden sign you've painted, a framed cross-stitch if you are crafty, or simply a chalkboard with the name written on it.)

a way to hang the sign near your candle

Optional extras:

an image of Vesta or her Greek counterpart, Hestia

The Rite

(In the following rite, the words in italics are there as examples, and you may substitute your own words as necessary.)

Begin by sweeping and vacuuming your house. In Rome, sweeping Vesta's temple was an important ritual, and while it is not necessary that you make your home's curb appeal perfect for this rite, sweeping and vacuuming is a way of showing that you have prepared and cleaned your space to welcome Vesta.

Gather everyone in your household together in your kitchen if possible. Light the candle (or turn it on if it's an LED) and place it in its new permanent spot in your kitchen.

Then speak aloud, "Vesta, guardian of the hearth and home, bright spot in our hearts who illuminates through the work of our hands, be welcome in this space. We wish to welcome you into our home, *Pinestead*. We are people who prize *love, creativity, courage, and hope*. We ask that you bring your warmth and protection into our home. We ask that you help us to make *Pinestead* a refuge *of art, joy, tranquility, and learning*, for us and for those whom the gods send to us as guests and friends. We welcome you in that spirit, that you may be part of our lives and part of our home, and that your blessings may extend to all who cross our threshold."

Now hang the sign somewhere in the kitchen where you will see it every day. If your candle is an LED, leave it on a timer so that it will glow every evening and remind you to thank Vesta. If it is a regular candle, remember to light it at least once a week and thank Vesta for her blessings upon your home. Reflect on those qualities that you asked Vesta to bring to your haven.

Once you have dedicated your haven, continue the work by allowing the gods to open your doors to those in need. Words are only words until intentions become actions. In deep Winter, it is your actions that will bring warmth to the world.

Warding Your Home

Sometimes your home needs a little more direct protection, whether from the stresses of the world or from the negativity of others. The Greeks and Romans had permanent protectors of the home at the entry points, doorkeepers whose job was to protect the inhabitants and their welcome guests. The Romans had a shrine called the *lararium,* dedicated to the *lares* and *penates,* that was usually located near the front door. These household deities worked with Vesta to protect the home.[54] The Greeks often had a pillar called a *herm* that stood outside the door, a square pillar with a man's head at the top and a man's genitals halfway down. The herm served a protective function as well, and its destruction or harm was seen as an impious attack on the family itself.[55]

For most of us today, having a shrine by the front door or a large phallic statue in our front yard is not possible. However, it is possible to create a house ward based on these principles.

Consider your space. While some people may be able to place something directly outside their front door, for apartment dwellers and others that may not be possible. Also, things that are on tables or shelves just inside the door may be moved or broken by children or pets. Painting or drawing directly on the doors may also not be possible—either because it will be too obviously Pagan to neighbors to have a big sigil painted on your door, or because you rent and are not allowed to paint. Wreaths or other décor hung on the door are wonderful, but generally need to be changed seasonally. Remember,

---

54. Bernstein, *Classical Living.*

55. Thucydides, *History of the Peloponnesian War* (New York: Penguin Classics, 1972).

the house ward needs to be permanent as long as you live in the home, not something temporary.

However, for most people, the one place near the door that will not be disturbed and is ideal for a protective function is the area right above the door on the inside between the doorframe and the ceiling. This is where, in some folk traditions, a horseshoe was hung for luck. You may, in fact, use a horseshoe. You may use some small piece of artwork that will fit, or even a sign painted on wood. A number of Pagan artisans on Etsy and other sites offer ceramic or resin plaques that are replicas of Roman votive plaques. There are also signs that read "Blessed Be" or "Love Lives Here" or other appropriate phrases. For those who practice in a Celtic tradition, there are Irish blessing plaques. If you are artistic, you may make your own, but it is fine to buy one if you prefer. The important thing is that it will fit over your door and seem natural in your home.

Once you have chosen what the physical component of your ward will be, you then need to charge it. (If you have multiple doors, you will want to have one physical component for each door and repeat this ritual for each.)

The Rite

You will need:

the plaque, horseshoe, sign, or other physical component you have chosen
a bowl (if your component is metal or ceramic, you may wish to use a bowl
   large enough to submerge it. If it is wood, paper, or another material that
   will be damaged, you will not submerge it, so a small bowl will do.)
water
sea salt
incense, preferably myrrh or sandalwood, and an incense holder
a means to light the incense

Begin at a central location in your house. A kitchen table is perfect, but you may choose to begin in any room. Fill the bowl with water. Add sea salt. Then light the incense. Say, "Pelagia, Sea Lady, Queen of Love, She Who Rules the Oceans of the World, whose saltwater runs through our veins as blood, whose breath touches us as rain, we humbly ask that you guard our home, keeping it safe from all dangers. We ask that you ward it safe so that only good intentions may pass our threshold. We ask that you guard it from injuries both spiritual and mundane. May we and those we welcome within these walls know no harm."

Place the component within the bowl of saltwater, or, if that is not possible, sprinkle it with the saltwater. Then light the incense. "Lady of the Seas, may your love and power touch every corner of our home."

Start at the front door, or the door that you are now warding if you have multiple doors. Lift the incense and its burner, letting the smoke touch the door and its area. Then begin walking *clockwise* around the interior of your home. You will need to go from room to room, but make sure you return each time to the exterior wall and let the smoke touch the exterior wall. What if, like my kitchen, you have cabinets that cover part of the exterior wall? Open each cabinet that backs on the exterior wall and let the smoke touch the back of the cabinets. Do the same with laundry areas, bathrooms, or other places where the exterior wall may be obscured. If your home is more than one story, do the story with the main door first, then work your way up and down. If, for example, you have a second floor and a basement, it does not matter whether you do the second story or the basement first as long as you do both. You want to cover all the space in your home that is lived in. You do not need to cover attics or crawl spaces since nobody is living there.

Once you have covered all the spaces, return to the door. Say, "Lady of the Sea, Venus Victrix, thank you for your protection."

If you have a second door, do that door next. If you have just covered the entire house, you do not need to take the smoke around again—just repeat your request and thanks to the Lady of the Sea and touch the smoke to that door.

Once you have completed your circuits, return to where your component(s) are at the kitchen table or whatever central place you are using. Say, "Sea Lady, Venus Victrix, let this be a symbol of your protection on our home." Then hang the component(s) above your door(s).

Allow the incense to burn out naturally.

Pour the saltwater outside in libation.

A Solid Place to Stand

Once your home is as safe and welcoming as it can be, a haven for all who seek it, you have a solid place to stand. Now that you have a refuge, it's time to think about the work you will do going forth from this place. As the Crisis era deepens, it's a time for heroes. What kind of hero will you be?

····· Chapter 10 ·····

Your Team of Heroes

Every team of heroes—whether it's a mythological band of Argonauts or a comic book superhero team or the crew of your favorite science fiction show—is made up of people with different abilities and skills who play different roles. Some are the diplomats and some are the warriors, some the healers and some the scientists. Some know lore and history, while others have technical expertise, street smarts, or skills at handling various weapons or emergencies. They're not all the same.

In this chapter, you'll choose what role you'll play on the team of heroes. There is a dedication ritual for each of the four paths, which follows a craft and rite in which you select your path. Remember, the team of heroes needs people in each path, and no path is more necessary or important than another. Each has its role to play and having people on each path is critical. It may be that among a coven, working group, or group of friends, almost everyone is on the same path. If, for example, you are a medical professional and most of your group is too, everyone may be a healer or a scientist. Rest assured there is another group out there in which everyone is a warrior! Together, we make up the vast tapestry of heroes in the universe we live in.

So what does it take to be a hero? What makes the good guys the good guys? We all learned this in comic books or from Harry Potter or Star Wars or the TV shows we watched when we were ten—the good guys are the ones who help people rather than hurt them. The heroes try to rescue, preserve, heal, and stop bad guys from hurting people. If that's what you're trying to do, you're a hero. You're on the team. However, if you enjoy cruelty and want to hurt people for the lulz, you're not on the team. Actually, you're a bad guy. You can reform and join the team, and that happens both in comics and in real life, but if you're enjoying making people miserable, feeling good about inciting hate, and laughing at suffering, these rituals aren't for you. This is about how good people come together to help.

Now, that doesn't mean they all agree about everything. That's another thing that hero stories tell us, whether ancient ones like the *Iliad* or modern ones like the Avengers. Good guys disagree. Heroes have arguments and sometimes want to whack each other on the side of the head, but at the end of the day they come together and face the threat together. We can disagree. We can disagree about strategy and tactics and where and when we should go and what we should prioritize, but when push comes to shove, heroes work together to save the world.

Choosing Your Role

You're in a museum. It's a crowded weekend afternoon, and the exhibit spaces are full of tourists and locals alike viewing the art and artifacts. Suddenly, there's a bang. You turn around and see flames and broken glass around one of the exhibit areas. People are screaming. There's blood on the floor, people stampeding in all directions. You see a man who seems to be holding two more Molotov cocktails. He turns and sprints into the next exhibit hall. What do you do?

A. I pull out my phone and start filming. The world needs to know what is happening here today.

B. I go after the man. Somebody's got to take him down before he does any more harm.

C. I try to help anyone who is injured. I get kids who don't seem to be with anyone to safety.

D. I grab the priceless art treasures nearest the flames and carry them to safety outside.

All of these are useful and good responses to the crisis. Which one you thought would best describe your reaction tells you what your natural role is in the Crisis era of saecular Winter.

If you chose A, your natural role is communicator. People can't make good decisions without good information. People can't form good opinions without knowing the truth.

If you chose B, your natural role is warrior. When threatened with physical danger, someone has to act physically to stop it, whether it's a bomber, an active shooter, or a natural disaster like a flood or hurricane.

If you chose C, your natural role is helper. People are bleeding, kids are lost and screaming, and someone needs to step in to help the people who are in crisis.

If you chose D, your natural role is conservator. Your job is to preserve treasures that are bigger than the present, or to conserve information—scientific, historic, artistic—that otherwise might be destroyed.

All of these things work together. Someone grabs the painting and someone else grabs the screaming toddler and both of them run out of the building. Someone goes after the guy with the Molotov cocktails and someone films it so that there is no misinformation about what happened. No one role is more important than another. These team positions are supposed to play together harmoniously.

Your role is defined not just by your temperament, but by your position in life and your skills. For example, I am a warrior by temperament, and had the Crisis era happened thirty years ago nothing would have made me happier than to go after the guy with the Molotov cocktail, but I am fifty-something and do not have the skills to go all *Die Hard*. Today, my actual skills are best served by being a helper. I can get those kids out of the building, stop people from panicking, and try to help the injured. Think about the role you would realistically play based on who you are today. What would you do in the museum scenario above?

Note there is not an option E—run over everyone on your way out the door and save your skin first. You are a hero. Heroes do not behave that way. There is also not an option F—lie on the floor and scream until someone saves you. What if no one does? In a Crisis era you have to take some action, even if it's only being responsible for your own evacuation.

Crafting a Commitment

In our society, one of the ways we symbolize a commitment is by wearing something special. Wedding rings are only one example. Medical professionals, clergy, fire and rescue, and others who have taken particular oaths often wear specific things as symbols of those oaths. These symbols serve to show others that they are committed, but there are also many symbols that are just for the person who is wearing them. For example, many people wear small or discreet symbols of their faith, while others wear headscarves or kippahs. Others wear mother's rings with a stone for each child, prayer beads, flag pins, rainbow jewelry, or even plastic bracelets that serve as reminders of their support of certain causes. This next craft is making a bracelet that symbolizes which of the four paths you are committing to.

You will need:

three eighteen-inch strands of cord. You may use silk, cotton, leather, or any other material you like. You will need three strands of the same type in three different colors. (If you mix different materials, like leather and silk, you will find it difficult to braid evenly.) See the following color chart for ideas about what colors to get. You may use different colors or several shades of the same one. Cord in different colors is available in most craft stores or online.

beads or charms that symbolize your intentions. These may be as simple or elaborate as you like. Make sure, however, that they will fit over the cords you have chosen. You may use any material, including shells with natural holes in them, metal, wood, stone, or ceramic. (Be certain that metal ones do not have sharp edges that will cut through the cord.) You can use just one or two, or many more if you prefer. If the holes are very large, you may put them over the braided strands of the finished bracelet rather than braiding them into the weave. You may also attach charms with jewelry rings, which are readily available in craft stores. You will need a small pair of pliers to open and close the rings if you use them.

Choosing your colors

Communicator	Warrior
yellow	red
white	black
gold	bronze
Helper	**Conservator**
blue	green
purple	brown
silver	copper

As an example, my bracelet has three strands of leather cord: a light teal and a dark teal and a purple, symbolizing my role as a helper who also conserves the lore of the past and tells stories for the present day. There are eight beads on it, all of which are blue or silver.

Another example belonging to someone else is two strands of silk cord, one green and one brown, and one strand of copper metallic cord. This bracelet has five wooden beads in different shapes and a copper charm of a treble clef to symbolize the conservator's vocation as a musician.

Making the bracelet

Once you've chosen your cords and your embellishments, tie your cords together near one end, leaving about two inches above the knot. At this point you're going to look at this and think this is much too long—after all, it's just got to slide over your hand! However as you begin to braid you will see how much the cord seems to shrink as the weave takes up length.

If you are putting the beads or charms on the cords, slip them on just before you snug the next piece in. If you plan to put the beads or charms on over the whole bracelet, braid it completely first.

Braid until you have a section that will not only go comfortably around your wrist, but will also slip over your hand to put it on. Some cords will give more than others, so hold the bracelet together and try slipping it on and off before you tie it. Once you have a comfortable fit, tie the free end of the braids together and cut off any cord in excess of two inches beyond the knot.

If you are slipping your beads over the full braid, put them on now. Then tie the bracelet to a comfortable fit and trim off any excess unbraided cord. You can wear the bracelet as a reminder of the course you have chosen, or you may put it on your home altar or somewhere else you will see it.

A Cycle of Rites of Dedication

In ancient times, rites were usually performed in cycles: a group of rites that together told an entire story or created an effect (for example, a journey and a return). Very rarely were rituals done in isolation, unconnected to a larger context.

A modern example of a cycle of rites is the Christian Holy Week following the season of Lent. Holy Week is a lunar festival, as many ancient festivals were, meaning that instead of occurring on a set date it differs each year depending on the moon. Easter is the culmination of Holy Week and is the first Sunday after the first full moon following Spring Equinox. Holy Week begins one week before, on Palm Sunday, which celebrates Jesus's arrival in Jerusalem. Next is Maundy Thursday, which commemorates the Last Supper and his betrayal. The next day is Good Friday, when Christians observe Jesus's death on the cross and burial in a tomb. Saturday is a solemn day of mourning, and Sunday, Easter, celebrates his resurrection. This is a very typical cycle of rites for the period and place in which this worship arose—in the Hellenistic world in the early Roman Empire. People would have found this cycle very familiar because it has much in common with older forms of worship. None of these rites are designed to be celebrated without the context of the full cycle. Together, they lead the worshiper through betrayal, death, descent, and return.

Thus, when we are looking at rites of dedication, particularly ones that are designed to help different people with different roles find their way in the team, the rites need to be connected. Hence, they are structurally similar and meant for a group to perform all four, not just one. Together, they create a full picture of responses to the crisis and complete the dedication of a team.

If you are solitary, you may skip the following section, as obviously you will perform only one as you are only one person. You will adapt the rite that is appropriate for you as needed to your situation.

Ancient festival dates often varied and it is not always possible for a modern group to keep to traditional dates. It's also difficult for some groups to do too many rites close together due to childcare, work schedules, and so on. However, there are two possibilities for putting a modern cycle together: the first spreads the rites out over a full festival season, and the second condenses them into a week.[56]

The first creates a cycle around our secular holidays from Memorial Day to the Fourth of July, celebrations that typically focus on the United States, its history, and its future. The cycle begins with Mercury on May 15, one of the ancient festival days for the god who rules over communication.

The second rite takes place on Memorial Day, the last Monday in May, when traditionally we celebrate those who have given their lives for the United States in the past. It's a fantastic time to continue the work of dedicating those who will protect and guide during the present crisis, honoring those who came before, and reaffirming that we continue their work through many forms of service. The second festival is Apollo's in his role as conservator and patron of arts, science, and learning—those things we strive to preserve.

The third rite is that of Diana Nemorensis on its traditional date of June 13. If you are unable for some reason to do the rite on that date, select the full moon of June instead.

---

56. The author is deeply grateful to Ivo Dominguez Jr. for his advice on the dates for certain rites.

The last rite honors Mars and is on July 4. It is appropriate to dedicate soldiers and first responders on this date because it celebrates the Declaration of Independence and the principles that they are called to serve.

Thus, the cycle is as follows:

May 15: Mercury

Memorial Day: Apollo

June 13: Diana Nemorensis

July 4: Mars

If you need to condense the rites into a week to perform them at a different time of year or to do them close together, it's recommended that you choose a week on the waxing moon with the last rite landing as close as possible to the full moon. Thus,

Wednesday: Mercury

Sunday: Apollo

Monday: Diana

Tuesday: Mars

If you are doing only one rite or feel that you need to do them at different times as events occur, there are also guidelines with each rite to help you plan.

Together these rites create a complete picture, with everyone able to find a rite that suits their role in the Crisis era. We will begin with Mercury.

Mercury

The Romans pictured Mercury as a young man often barely out of his teens, a fleet-footed youth who delivered messages faster than the wind. He was often portrayed wearing winged boots to show how fast he traveled.

It's easy to characterize the role of communicator as simply about passing on information, and that's true, but there is more to it than that. Today, we are swimming in a sea of information. As attention turns to fake news and deepfakes, what we need most is to know the truth. We need means of separating accusations from facts, wishful thinking from actual events, and rumors from news. One of the functions of the communicator is to tell the truth. Sometimes that's saying things the mainstream won't. Often it's pointing out that something is unsubstantiated. After all, today anyone can say anything and have it go viral.

How do you tell which source to trust? How do you know whose information is real? In a crisis situation like a hurricane making landfall, having real information about storm strength, evacuation routes, and timing may make the difference between your family's survival and you being a sad statistic. In a disaster, the rumor that a certain place is safe for evacuees when it isn't can cost lives. Imagine this scenario—a hurricane is battering New York with high winds, blowing out windows of high-rise buildings and making furnishings into projectiles. The rumor spreads online that people are instructed to take shelter in subway stations. And then the tunnels fill with water, as they did in Superstorm Sandy. Water pours in torrents down staircases, and lights go out as power lines short. Imagine what is happening in those tunnels in the dark, cold water. That is the cost of rumor. That is the cost of misinformation.

You need the truth. Mercury is not just about information, but true information. When you dedicate yourself to Mercury, you are pledging to provide truth—whether that means only retweeting bulletins from reliable weather sources, debunking misinformation, or refusing to spread rumors.

The other side of communication is advocacy, the war of words. Rhetoric, persuasion, debate, and reasoned argument are Mercury's gifts. Those who advocate for peaceful change are also communicators. Attorneys, nonviolent activists, writers, and other "opinion leaders" are communicators. These are powerful roles. They must be undertaken with responsibility and due concern for the very real changes they make in people's lives. Who has custody of a child? Who has the right to live where? Who goes to jail and who goes free? Whom should people vote for? Who moves people to act or cease acting? At its zenith, the communicator has the power of Martin Luther King Jr. and commensurate responsibility.

Of course this role has a dark side: the demagogue who stirs up outrage for power and attention. Maybe they're a radio personality with millions of listeners. Maybe they're a blogger with dozens. Maybe they're rich and famous. Maybe they're you. The role of advocate, of communicator, comes with responsibility. Just as the first side of Mercury's role is truth, the second is responsibility. Are you urging people to actions that are beneficial? That are helpful to them and to others? Or are you shirking responsibility, saying it doesn't really matter what you say, that you're just being ironic? It matters. Just as untruthful information can cost lives, advocacy based on hate or irresponsibility can destroy them. This rite asks Mercury to grant his gifts of truth and responsibility to those who take up the role of communicator.

This rite should be performed on May 15, one of Mercury's traditional festival days. You will need two officiants to lead the ritual. They may be any gender, but they should be mature and thoughtful communicators.

You will need:
yellow candles (a large one for the altar and as many smaller candles as you
    wish—at least one for each person who is asking for Mercury's blessing)
a means to light the candles
an incense burner and incense (lavender or rosemary is ideal)
a goblet of white wine and a libation bowl

Optional extras:
a statue or image of Mercury
a vase of mixed flowers (iris and daffodil are particularly appropriate)
a white or yellow altar cloth
symbols of the service of those who are asking for a blessing, including their
    (silenced) phones

The Rite

OFFICIANT ONE: Swift Mercury, bringer of news, clear speaker and friend of humanity, we call upon you tonight. [Light the large yellow candle, then all of the others except one each for the people who are seeking Mercury's blessing.]

OFFICIANT TWO: Bright messenger, help us to speak bravely, truthfully, tactfully, and at the proper time. We know that the wrong words can harm, and that we are responsible for what we say just as we are responsible for what we do. [Light the incense.]

OFFICIANT ONE: If I urge a man to avenge himself and he harms the innocent, am I not also culpable?

OFFICIANT TWO: If I persuade a woman to do something that is harmful to her, am I not also culpable?

OFFICIANT ONE: If I claim to speak with authority and I lie, am I not culpable?

OFFICIANT TWO: If I accuse the innocent, am I not culpable?

OFFICIANT ONE: Mercury, healer of bodies, voice of truth, help us to speak with restraint so that our words are measured and reasonable.

OFFICIANT TWO: Mercury, bright star of morning, help us to speak with courage so that our words inspire others.

OFFICIANT ONE: Words are power.

OFFICIANT TWO: Words are strength.

OFFICIANT ONE: Words are healing.

OFFICIANT TWO: Words are truth.

OFFICIANT ONE: Help us all, who dedicate our lives to communication, to speak powerfully, truthfully, and compassionately.

If the officiants are themselves on the path of communicators, they should go first and set an example of how to make the dedication. Each person who is on this path should make their dedication separately and aloud, and then light one of the yellow candles. For example, "Mercury, I am asking for your blessing on my work as a camera operator for the local news. Please help me provide accurate and helpful information to my community." Another example: "Mercury, I am asking for your blessing on my work on political campaigns.

Please help me be truthful, articulate, and work toward the greatest good for the greatest number of people." Another example: "Mercury, I am asking for your blessing on my work as a fundraiser for an organization that fights cancer. Help me speak convincingly and compassionately so that people can benefit from the work that we do." There are many different ways that people may be on the path of the communicator, so make sure each person has plenty of time to think about and decide what they are going to say before the ritual. This is definitely not a one-size-fits-all dedication!

When everyone who is making a dedication has had a chance to speak, officiant two steps forward.

OFFICIANT TWO: God of Bright Blessings, we thank you for your aid, now and in the years to come. [Pour a libation into the bowl.]

OFFICIANT ONE: We know your power. We know the power in each impulse shooting through the ether, each fast-as-light bit of information running on your winged feet. Help us use this power wisely, for wisdom also is yours. You transform torrents of facts into useful stories. Grant us that wisdom. Help us heal our world through the power of words.

OFFICIANT TWO: Thank you. May all assembled here go forth in your clarity.

You may allow the candles and incense to burn while you share refreshments according to your tradition, or you may put them out right away. Each person who did the dedication should take their candle home with them as a reminder of their promises. The libation bowl should be emptied outside if that is possible.

Apollo

Apollo is the protector of the works of people, of civilization. Apollo preserves the things that people need to thrive, including medicine and the sciences, music and visual arts, law and architecture. These are the things that eras of crisis put at risk. Cities are destroyed, infrastructure crumbles, buildings burn with all their furniture and handicrafts and clothes and electronics and all that we hold precious. Power flickers out. Water taps give nothing but brown sludge. Food doesn't arrive at markets, not through flooded tunnels or over destroyed bridges. Smashed musical instruments sit in the rubble of a school, torn pages of books blowing away in the wind. Apollo is the preserver of all these things, the things that humans create that make life safe, comfortable, and happy. If your role is a conservator, your patron in this work is Apollo.

"Keep Calm and Carry On" was a slogan the British used during World War II that sums up perfectly the conservator's work. No matter what is going on in the world, the water system needs to keep working. The groceries need to be restocked as best as they can be and the store needs to be open with the registers working. Schools need to be open if they safely can be because children don't stop growing for the four or five years of a Crisis era. People still need flu shots and dental cleanings. They still need tires for their cars and kibble for their cats. And, even in the most terrible times, people need joy. They need music and beauty and all the things that make life precious. These are not frivolous things. Art and love and joy are what lift us up, and the darker things are, the more we need to be lifted and illuminated.

The conservator's job is to make sure that civilization endures. After all, a saecular Crisis era is a relatively short time in the history of the world. Consider the people who carefully packed ancient artifacts from the British Museum and hid them down coal mines in Wales during World War II. For them, this was the work of a lifetime. For the statues, this was four years out of the more than two thousand they have endured. And yet if they had been destroyed, what a tragedy it would have been! There will be an afterward. The conservator makes sure that precious things are still here when it's over and preserves the ordinary, day-to-day functions of society as much as possible during the Crisis era.

This rite should be celebrated on Memorial Day, which is the last Monday in May. It is the day we remember those who have died in the service of the United States; therefore, it is an appropriate time to request Apollo's help to continue their work of conserving the things we hold dear. It's important that this rite be during the day rather than at night because of Apollo's relationship with Helios, the sun.

If you are doing this rite alone, simply speak the parts for the officiant and the dedicant both.

You will need:
white candles (a large one for the altar and as many smaller candles as you
   wish—at least one for each person who is asking for Apollo's blessing)
matches
an incense burner and incense (laurel or bay is preferred)
a goblet of red wine and a libation bowl
More wine (or another beverage if you prefer something nonalcoholic) for
   sharing

Optional extras:
a statue or image of Apollo
bay leaves or laurel leaves to dress the altar
musical instruments or instruments of craft—paintbrushes, measuring tapes,
   or even calculators
a white altar cloth
gold-colored anything (it is especially appropriate to use gold-colored can-
   dleholders, bowls, goblets, or any other vessels in respect to Apollo's solar
   aspect)

The Rite

Choose a room where there is either little natural light or where you can draw curtains to block out outside daylight. You want to begin in near darkness. In the darkness, everyone waits silently until the officiant is ready to begin.

OFFICIANT: [Strike a match and light the incense, then put the match out. Speak slowly and quietly.] In darkness, there is mystery. In darkness, in the bay-scented smoke of the darkest cave, Apollo speaks to Pythia. He whispers. In darkness, we wait.

Again the officiant should wait, letting the incense burn until it begins to seem like a long time, though it is probably only a minute or two. Then light the large white candle.

OFFICIANT: Proud Helios, Apollo who returns with the dawn, light in darkness, we greet you. Grant your blessings to us this day. We come to you in a time of trouble, when so much of the knowledge of humanity is at risk, when so much of the work of our hands stands in jeopardy. God of civilization, who gives us books and paintings, mathematics and biochemistry, air-conditioning and smartphones, help us to preserve all that is valuable to us in this time of crisis. Some of us who stand here are dedicated to preserving particular parts of the gathered wisdom of humanity and the vital fabric of life. Let us join our lights with yours.

Each person who is asking for Apollo's blessing will come forward and light one of the smaller white candles off the main candle. They will speak, in their own words, their request for help with their particular work. Some examples: "Let me be a light in the world by preserving and teaching scientific knowledge. As a high school biology teacher, I transmit important knowledge to a new generation. Help me preserve this knowledge by passing it on." "Let me be a light in the world through my work as a volunteer docent at Local Historical House. Help me to preserve this architectural treasure and teach future generations about how our ancestors lived and thought." "Let me be a light in the world through my work as a water treatment plant operator for Local Water and Sewer Company. Help me to make sure that our community continues to have clean, safe drinking water no matter what is going on in the world around us." There are many more possible examples, as this is the broadest of the four categories. Let each person speak according to their own heart.

When everyone has had a chance to speak, the officiant should open the curtains or doors to other rooms and let in as much natural daylight as possible.

OFFICIANT: Apollo, bright and penetrating light, help us to do these things that we have promised. Keep us faithful to our charges. Guide us to act with wisdom and restraint. [Pour a libation in wine.] We do your work, preserving the achievements of those who came before us and contributing to the building of the world. Help us to be a bulwark against chaos, that all that is precious may survive and come forth with us into day. We thank you.

Each of the participants, including those who did not ask for Apollo's blessing specifically on their work, may provide thanks for whatever they wish. Some examples: "Thank you for recorded music so that everyone can enjoy it." "Thank you for HVAC engineers and technicians so that our homes and workplaces can be warm in winter and cool in summer." "Thank you for UPS, which delivers my packages." "Thank you for libraries so that everyone can read books and learn." "Thank you for injectable insulin, which keeps me alive." "Thank you for chocolate, which brings us so much happiness." They can be very serious or simply joyful. Remember, beauty and happiness are not frivolous. They are the reason we keep going—the promise of light at the end of the tunnel, the promise that life is not just a grim slog until you drop, exhausted and used up. We need joy. The officiant should try to steer the thanks more toward joy as people speak.

OFFICIANT: We give thanks for the privilege of being part of this great work. [Pour more wine or another beverage into the goblet.] Wine has long been a symbol of civilization. It is the perfect melding of nature and craft, of cultivation and skill, of weather and happy accident and long experience. When we share it, we partake of something humans have enjoyed for thousands of years. We share the gift of that liminal place between Apollo and Dionysus, where reason meets emotion and science meets art. Share with us now, and give thanks.

The officiant drinks and then passes the goblet *clockwise* around the circle and everyone takes a sip. If there is still more in the goblet when it returns to the officiant, they may pour the rest in libation.

OFFICIANT: We go forth, and Apollo goes with us.

You may let the candles burn while you break for a meal or other refreshments. The smaller candles should be taken home by the people who lit them as reminders of their requests.

Diana Nemorensis

Apollo has a twin sister, Diana. One of her symbols is the hound. Companion of hunters, herders, and travelers in dangerous places, the hound is the friend of humanity, perhaps its dearest friend. Anyone who has known the love of a dog knows that there is no purer love. Long ago, before people had fields and crops and cattle, dogs were our first friends. We were their pack, or they were ours—companions on the hunt. With a dog, the hunters can run down large prey: deer and boar that are too swift or too dangerous to face without a fleet and fierce companion. And when the hunt is over, the hound sleeps beside the fire of those she loves, a gentle and loving friend to children, to the elderly, and to all who are part of her pack.

The Romans had an important shrine at Lake Nemi just south of Rome that was dedicated to Diana Nemorensis. This shrine was magnificent, set on the shore of a perfectly round lake known as Diana's Mirror. A natural remnant of an ancient volcanic caldera, it reflected the night sky in its cold, pure water. Around it the forests belonged to the shrine and were kept untouched because they belonged to Diana of the Forest, she who guards and protects humans who go into the wild. The shepherd who seeks his lambs on dangerous, broken ground has his dog beside him, and likewise the traveler who journeys far from home. The midwife called out in the middle of the night to a remote farm walks with her dog at her side, and the lost child is found by the keen nose of the hound. Today the search and rescue dog hunts for survivors of an earthquake and the service dog assists those with special needs. Diana Nemorensis is the guardian of those who help.

Usually Diana Nemorensis is depicted as a beautiful young woman—or three women to show her triple nature as the moon goddess, the huntress, and the guardian of the doors to the underworld, a role that associates her with Hecate. She was also represented by a white doe or a white hound, and Diana's hounds could pursue the evildoer and bring them to justice. In the story of Actaeon, her hounds tore apart the man who had spied on her and her virgin attendants bathing naked. However, more often she was invoked as a protector than avenger, especially of children, young women, the elderly, and those who were helpless.

The ritual that follows is designed to ask for Diana Nemorensis's blessing and aid upon those whose role is to help others. This rite can be performed either alone or with a group. If it is with a group, only those who have chosen the role of helper should ask for Diana's blessing, as the role comes with responsibilities. Others in the group presumably have chosen other roles and will do the rites appropriate for them.

Before the rite, those who intend to ask for Diana's blessing should think about exactly what their role entails and be prepared to say it at the appropriate point. The traditional date of Diana Nemorensis's festival is June 13, but you may choose the night of any full moon. If you are doing this rite alone, simply speak the parts for the officiant and the dedicant both.

You will need:
dark blue candles (a large one for the altar and as many smaller candles as
  you wish—at least one for each person who is asking for Diana's blessing)
a means to light the candles
an incense burner and incense (cedar, pine, or another forest scent is preferred)
a goblet of white wine and a libation bowl
a bowl of fresh strawberries (The wild strawberries of Lake Nemi are
  famous, and even today the Lake Nemi Strawberry Festival involves a
  procession of young girls in white dresses with red ribbons.)[57]
a round mirror

Optional extras:
a statue or image of Diana
an image or statue of a dog (preferably a hound, though any dog will do)

---

57. "Nemi Strawberry Festival near Rome," DeliciouslyItaly.com, August 31, 2010,
    https://www.deliciousitaly.com/lazio-rome-itineraries/nemi-strawberry-festival-near-rome.

evergreen branches of any kind (fir, pine, cedar, or even magnolia)

a white altar cloth

a dog (If you have a well-behaved dog, it is perfectly appropriate to have
them at your side in this rite.)

Silver or silver-colored anything (it is especially appropriate to use silver can-
dleholders, bowls, goblets, or any other vessels in respect to Diana's lunar
aspect)

The Rite

Set up your altar with the altar cloth and the evergreen branches if you are
using them. Place the image of Diana and/or the image of a hound in the
center. Place the largest blue candle in front. Cluster the other blue candles
around with the incense and burner. Put the goblet of wine and the libation
bowl on one side and the bowl of strawberries on the other. Place the mirror
front and center so that the candlelight will reflect in its surface.

Gather quietly before the altar and turn off any nearby electric lights that
will be distracting. You want a twilight level of light once the candles are lit.

OFFICIANT: Diana Nemorensis, Lady of the Forest, protector of those who
serve others, be with us tonight. [Light the largest blue candle, then all of the
others except one each for the people who are seeking Diana's blessing. Then
light the incense.] We are asking for your blessing tonight upon those who do
your work, who are your hands, helping others and caring for other people
and for other living creatures. We are asking for your blessing on [name,
name, and name]. May the first of you come forward.

The first person who is asking for Diana's blessing comes forward and
speaks directly to the goddess, as though they were introducing themselves
based on the work they have already considered asking her to bless. Some
examples: "I am asking for your blessing on my work as a nurse so that I may
be better prepared to save lives"; "I would like your blessing on my work as
a social worker so that I can better serve the children who come into my
care"; and "I would like your blessing on my work as an insurance adjuster

so that I can better help people who have lost their homes and possessions to fires, storms, and other disasters." Remember, it does not have to be work they do for a living. They may also help others as a volunteer. "I am asking for your blessing on my work as a CERT volunteer in my community." "I request your blessing in training service dogs and your blessing for the dogs I train." Their words may be as long or as short as they wish. When they have finished, they light one of the blue candles and the officiant speaks.

OFFICIANT: Diana Nemorensis has a lake so clear it is known as Diana's Mirror. A full moon reflects on it so clearly that it seems the moon shines up from the bottom of the lake. Look into Diana's Mirror. You will see her face looking up, her representative and her hands.

The person asking for the blessing leans over and looks in the mirror surrounded by candles. Of course it is their own face they see. They are Diana's representative.

OFFICIANT: May Her blessing be upon you.

That person steps back and the next comes to take their place. Repeat until all who seek Diana's blessing have had their turn. This may be very emotional for the participants. If so, allow it to be. Compassion and love are often accompanied by tears and embraces. Let it be what it is. When everyone has had their turn, the officiant speaks again.

OFFICIANT: Lady of the Forest, Diana Nemorensis, thank you for your blessings on those who serve others. Help them to guide, protect, and give hope to those in need. May your light shine through them. Thank you. [Lift the bowl of strawberries.] Let us share in the sweetness of Diana's grace. [Pass the bowl around the circle, each person who wishes to taking a strawberry and eating it. Place the bowl back on the altar.] We go in peace, filled with your love. [Put out the central candle and the incense.]

The other candles may be allowed to burn while the group breaks for refreshments of some sort. It's recommended that you do so to help everyone ground, though what kind of food you have is up to you. You may have a full potluck dinner, just snacks, or cakes and ale if your tradition calls for them.

After people have eaten, the smaller candles can be extinguished for the participants to take home as reminders of their dedication. The libation and any remaining strawberries should be put outside.

Mars

Just as there is a time for peace, there is a time for war. While we do not seek it—particularly not the bloody war of brother on brother that is civil war—like the Romans, we know that it comes. The fire of ekpyrosis burns in its time. Just as there is a time to lay down arms, there is a time to take them up. This ritual is for those who are literally taking up arms, who are preparing to kill if necessary, or to die in protection of the community. This is not advocacy or the war of words. This is physical combat, the role of the soldier, the person whose job it is to step into harm's way, to take down the active shooter at the mall, to go into the burning building that may collapse, to plunge into the storm surge to get someone into a helicopter basket. This ritual is for our society's warriors.

The Roman god of war, Mars, is usually depicted as a mature man with a beard, helmet, armor, and a long spear. He is not a beautiful and rash youth. He is old enough to understand the fearsome responsibility he undertakes, to guard the community with his strength, his blood, and if necessary his life. For the first four hundred years of the city, there was no temple to Mars within the walls of Rome. He is a god of wild places, and his animal is the wolf, that consummate pack hunter who kills as part of a team and who lives in a complex social order. Mars is the wolf. He stalks the boundaries, living beyond the pale of the civilized city that he and his band of brothers guard with their lives. Remember as well that while military service was the prov-ince solely of men among the Romans, wolves are hunters, male and female alike. The wolf pack does not exclude females, and Mars does not exclude females from his worship.

Mars was celebrated at an open-air altar outside the walls on the *Campus Martius*, the parade ground where military training was held and where soldiers mustered while either leaving for war or returning. As there are today, there were military ceremonies there to induct soldiers into service, to promote or award those who had distinguished themselves, and to remember those who had fallen. The complexity of those ceremonies is beyond the scope of this book, but the thrust of them is twofold: honor and valor accrue to the brave, honorable soldier, while at the same time those who shed blood are set apart. They are not the same as the ordinary citizen, and ritual is required to step into that state and return from it.

The ritual that follows is designed to hallow and bless those who take up the arms of Mars. Some will literally take up weapons as soldiers, while others will be police, first responders, volunteers, or those who put themselves in harm's way in defense of the community. This ritual is designed for a group in which one or more people are taking this step. There is also a variation to ask for Mars's blessing on loved ones who are not able to be present.

This rite should be performed on July 4, the day when Americans celebrate the signing of the Declaration of Independence, our first compact and commitment to the principles of liberty. If there is a member who is a veteran or a seasoned first responder or a soldier, they should act as officiant. Otherwise, the officiant should be a mature person.

You will need:

red candles (a large one for the altar and as many smaller candles as you wish—at least one for each person who is asking for Mars's blessing. More candles rather than fewer is better.)

a means to light the candles

an image or statue of a wolf (plus an additional one for each person asking for Mars's blessing, preferably small enough to put in a pocket or a pendant that can be worn on a necklace)

an incense burner and incense (dragon's blood, sandalwood, or pine is preferred)

a goblet of red wine and a libation bowl

Optional extras:

a statue or image of Mars

pieces of carnelian

a vase of red and white carnations

a red altar cloth (or red, white, and blue if appropriate)

symbols of the service those who are asking for a blessing perform—badges,
    medals, etc.

The Rite

Set up your altar with the altar cloth and flowers if you are using them. Place
the large image of a wolf and/or the image of Mars in the center. Place the
largest red candle in front and cluster around it the other candles, the pieces
of carnelian, the smaller wolf images, and the incense and burner. Place the
symbols of service among them if you are using them. Put the goblet of
wine and the libation bowl in front of the candles and images.

Gather quietly before the altar.

OFFICIANT: Father of Wolves, He who leads the pack, Mars of the bloody
spear, warrior and defender, today we call upon you. [Light the large red candle, then all of the others except one each for the people who are seeking
Mars's blessing. Then light the incense.] We make offering to you as people
have for thousands of years, to ask that you hallow our warriors who fight
for us, keep them safe in their travails, and return them to us in due course
of time.

GROUP: We ask your blessing upon [insert name(s) of those seeking the
blessing].

OFFICIANT: You enter into a Mystery belonging to the gods. You put your-
selves forward as the sacrifice, your blood to be spilled if necessary. You put
yourself in great peril, not just in peril of death, but of injury and pain. You
will be forever changed.

If the officiant is a veteran or an experienced servant of Mars, they should
talk about what this service has meant to them, how it has changed them,

and what this Mystery is in their lives. If there are others in the group who also have served this way, they should also share their experiences. Needless to say, those who have not should not interject—they are not initiates of this Mystery and it is inappropriate.

PERSON WHO IS NONINITIATE: In ancient times, those who guarded the boundaries from peril had the blessing of the community. We ask you to guard us. We ask you to remember that the service you are consecrated to is the service of home. You serve the weak, the young, the old, the vulnerable. You protect those who cannot protect themselves from whatever hazards may come, whether those hazards be natural or man-made. We are grateful to you, for you guard us.

OFFICIANT: Do you [names] pledge yourself to the service of Mars freely and without reservation, to be the wolf pack that guards the boundaries, to serve with honor and courage, to take up the mantle of heroes of our community?

DEDICANTS: We so swear.

OFFICIANT: Do you swear to act with integrity and loyalty to those who depend on you, to serve truth, justice, and all that is best in the community that loves you and sends you forth as its champion?

DEDICANTS: We so swear.

EACH DEDICANT SEPARATELY: May Mars help me fulfill my vow. [Add additional vows as desired. Light one of the remaining red candles, then pour a solemn libation to Mars from the wine goblet to the libation bowl.] Take this wine in token of my blood, shed if it must be in defense of my home and those I love.

OFFICIANT: [Wait until each person has done their vows. Take up a wolf token for each person] Mars, Mavors, Genitor, Gradivus, Quirinus, Pater, Silvanius, Ultor, bless these dedicants who take up your service, as others have since the dawn of time. Stand with them in the shield line and be with them in the watches of the night. Grant them courage, honor, judgment, and wisdom in what they do. Grant them valor and restraint. Grant them wily cleverness and brave honesty. Lead your wolves so that they may guard our community. We garland them as our champions. We send them forth with our blessings and yours. Mars, be with them. And bring them safely home when the storm is past. [Give a wolf token to each.] Take these blessed amulets as a symbol of your charge.

DEDICANTS: [Take the tokens with thanks.]

OFFICIANT: Mars, Wolf-father, thank you for your attention and your blessings. Now we shall honor our champions.

Allow the incense and candles to burn while you serve a meal in honor of the dedicants. This can be a potluck, can be celebratory rather than solemn, and can include people who were not part of the rite, like children too young for the serious rite or other loved ones who are not Pagan. After the meal, the officiant should extinguish the candles and put them somewhere safe, as well as pour the libations outside on the ground. The dedicants can help with this if they wish.

Variation if the dedicants can't be present

This variation on the rite is appropriate if the people who are being called to serve are not able to be present. For example, someone has already been deployed and is far away, or someone's son isn't sure about this stuff. This is asking for a blessing upon those who serve rather than being an oath-taking for them.

Set up the altar as above, only add photographs of those whom you seek Mars's blessing upon.

OFFICIANT: Father of Wolves, He who leads the pack, Mars of the bloody spear, warrior and defender, today we call upon you. [Light the large red candle, then all of the others except one each for the people who are seeking Mars's blessing. Then light the incense.] We make offering to you as people have for thousands of years, to ask that you hallow our warriors who fight for us, keep them safe in their travails, and return them to us in due course of time. We ask for your blessings upon [insert names], that they may know your protection and may serve with valor and honor. As I name each person again, would someone who asks for blessing on their behalf come forth? [Say the dedicant's first name.]

PERSON REPRESENTING THAT PERSON: [Light a red candle on their behalf.] Mars, Father of Wolves, please keep [name] safe, and help them do their duty with honor, compassion, and courage. [Add whatever additional prayer you wish, and then pour a libation in wine on behalf of the person.]

OFFICIANT: [When they have finished, select one of the wolf tokens and give it to them.] May this token symbolize the blessing of Mars, Father of Wolves, and his protection upon [name].

This repeats until all the people who seek blessings have had their turn.

OFFICIANT: Mars, Mavors, Genitor, Gradivus, Quirinus, Pater, Silvanius, Ultor, bless these who take up your service, as others have since the dawn of time. Stand with them in the shield line and be with them in the watches of the night. Grant them courage, honor, judgment, and wisdom in what they do. Grant them valor and restraint. Grant them wily cleverness and brave honesty. Lead your wolves so that they may guard our community. We garland them as our champions. We send them forth with our blessings and yours. Mars, be with them. And bring them safely home when the storm is past.

Break now for a meal together. It may be a potluck or more elaborate as you like. Allow the candles and incense to burn until the meal is ending. The persons who asked for blessings on behalf of others should take the candles, their photographs, and the wolf tokens home for them. If the people who asked for the blessing think it's appropriate, they may send the wolf tokens to the people they were hallowed for. The other candles should be put away safely. The libation should be poured outside.

These rites may be very emotional, and they should be. This is about sending forth our champions to guard the community, knowing that their danger is real and that they are standing in harm's way on our behalf. This is profound. It should be deeply emotional. Don't be upset or ashamed if it is. Embrace it. That is what this is.

The Team Gathers

As the storm deepens, we each play our part. We each serve one another, stick together, are brave and work hard, and live our values. We were born for this, and we can do it, just as millions have before us. We are not feeble creatures. We were born to face the storms.

The Aftermath

Chapter 11

The Storm Wanes

The time will come when the storm has waned. The time will come when Winter is almost over. Sometime around 2025, if the pattern of the saecula holds true, we will come to the end of the Crisis era. This is the point when we say to ourselves, both as individuals and as a people, "Okay, what happens next?"

An era has ended. It's time for a new one to begin. It may be hard to move on from Winter no matter how challenging it has been. This meditation is designed to help you leave Winter behind so that you may begin the next season.

Meditation: Ice Melt

For this meditation you will need an ice cube and a bowl of warm water. If you wish to play soothing instrumental music, you may. If you are doing the exercises in this book with others, you may wish for someone to read the following passage aloud. Otherwise you may simply read it to yourself.

Put the ice cube in the bowl of water. As you read, watch how at first it bobs to the surface and then begins to get smaller and smaller.

———— • ————

In winter, the world is locked in ice. Rivers and streams are frozen, their music stilled. The banks are encased in snow. Cold winds blow.

At night, the stars are pale and cold above the frozen waters, shining all the more brightly on the surface of the ice.

So too we are frozen in Winter, locked in the harsh realities of our world. We cannot move. We cannot become; not yet.

The night is cold. The ice covers the river, but beneath the surface currents are moving. Down in the depths, below the scoured surface, fish are stirring. The water is warming. Each day it warms a little more. Each day the ice thins a little bit.

Upstream somewhere, it rains. It may be ten miles away. It may be a hundred. But it rains. Warm water flows off streets and parking lots and houses, cascades down storm drains. Into streams. Into the river.

The stars are bright over the ice, and suddenly the stillness is broken by a great *crack!* Maybe you can see it. Maybe it's beneath the surface, but the ice breaks. *Crack!* It's a sound like tree limbs snapping, like cables tearing apart. *Crack!* There it is again.

And now you see it. The ice is moving.

The warm water beneath is carrying it. *Crack!* Another piece breaks.

Suddenly, the surface isn't solid. It's a bunch of ice floes, bumping and tossing against one another, jumbling downstream.

The river is free. No longer locked in winter, no longer bound by ice, the river sings again.

Each obstruction, each rapid or stone, speeds the breaks. Great pieces crumble as they leap down into the pools beneath. Little chunks float on the surface, diminishing as you watch.

Winter has ended. The ice has broken. It may not yet be spring, but it is no longer winter.

So too have we reached a place in the great year when it is no longer Winter. Spring will come soon. The ice is melting.

———— • ————

Continue to watch the ice until it has completely disappeared. Know in your heart that Winter is over.

Opening the Mundus Cereris

Consider the seed you stored back in the beginning of the Crisis era. Now is the time to bring it forth and think about how and when you will plant these seeds. Since every person will have a different collection of ideas, treasures, and institutions, exactly how you plant the seeds will be different. Some people may create based on the cultural treasures they preserved. Others may run for office in hopes of conserving or reinstituting programs or laws that they considered of surpassing worth. Still others may continue work interrupted—scientific or sociological research, artistic endeavors, or other forms of work that were disrupted by the events of the last few years. You may know exactly which seeds you want to plant on the first day of the new saeculum. Or you may have completely forgotten what you wrote on those little pieces of paper five years ago—that is also okay.

It may be obvious when it's time to open the mundus cereris. The end of World War II was known to everyone—a national day of spontaneous celebration. Or it may not be obvious—conflicts may seem to trickle to a halt, problems may begin to resolve slowly so that one day it strikes you, "Hey, that problem hasn't happened in a while." A month? Two months? What day is it really Spring? When you know that it is, it's time to open the gates of the underworld again—time for Proserpina to ascend with your seeds in her arms.

In the ancient world, this was one of the great mysteries. Life seems to have ended. And then it begins again. The Greater Eleusinian Mysteries were a complete cycle of holy days and celebrations around the return of the Lady of the Dead to the world above to become once again the spring maiden. While a full look at the mystery cycle is beyond the scope of this book, we consider her as the keeper of seed—one of her chthonic faces—and therefore, we must reclaim the seed from her. (If you do not have the jar or pot from the previous ritual, there is a variation that follows.)

The Rite

Now we are prepared to open the mundus cereris and prepare for Spring.

You will need:
the jar or pot that you prepared in the previous ritual
an apple
a glass of white wine or apple juice
a white candle
a burner and incense, preferably patchouli, sandalwood, or myrrh

Optional extras:
calendars, datebooks, or planners from 2019 through the present day
an image of Father Dis and Proserpina

Begin by lighting the incense. As you do so, imagine Father Dis as the winter king, an old man with flowing white hair wearing a rich robe of dark cloth, its borders worked with gold thread. He sits on a throne, and about him are all the hidden treasures of the underworld.

Say, "Father Dis, you have kept the seed in your treasury. You have protected it through all of winter's toils. Thank you." The incense is your offering to him. Let it burn for a moment, closing your eyes and imagining the deep, safe places where he has kept this seed for you.

Say, "Now it is spring, and it is time for your lady to return to us. Lady—Queen—Proserpina—please return to us with the spring, that these seeds may quicken."

Imagine her, golden hair now loose on her shoulders, a circlet of spring flowers on her head. Clad in her white gown, she bids farewell to her husband and king, a parting that is of course temporary, for she will return to him with the turning of the seasons. She carries your jar of seeds in her arms as she turns and walks toward you. Behind her, the Gates of Horn close, shutting away the world below and disappearing. Where her feet touch, flowers spring up, the world greening at her approach. Smiling, she hands you the jar.

Say, "Thank you, bright lady," and open the jar.

Inside are your slips of paper and the snakes you put with them, just as you left them years ago. Light the white candle for Proserpina and sit down. One by one, take them out and read them.

If you have calendars, datebooks, or planners from 2019 through the present day, open them up as well. Read through them. Remember who you were and what you were doing. Some of the entries will fill you with delight. Oh remember that! That was wonderful. Others will fill you with sadness. Perhaps they are times that you spent with people who are now gone. Perhaps they are places you wonder if you will ever go to again—places that may have irrevocably changed. Perhaps you will see doctor's appointments before your child was born, or perhaps there are vet appointments for a pet who died two years ago. Perhaps there are vacations or plans with people you love. Or perhaps there are plans with people you love who you will never see again. Remember. Weep. Laugh. Absorb the changes that have happened to you since you stored this seed.

Then look at the seeds again. What did you value? What do you still value? What did you believe was in peril that has survived admirably? What did you wish to keep that you fear has been swept away? What do you look at and wonder what you were thinking when you wrote it? What do you look at with a smile?

Which seeds do you wish to plant? Organize them into two piles: the ones you wish to plant and the ones you don't. It's okay if most of them are ones you wish to plant. After all, you chose these things because you thought they were important, and very probably, five years or so later, you still do.

Now examine the ones you wish to plant. Choose three or four that you will take action on now. This can be complicated, like working for voting rights for everyone, or as simple as reminding people of a story or music that you love. But take action. Plan how you will plant these seeds. Imagine what will come of them five years from now when they have taken root.

Cut the apple and offer half to Proserpina. Say, "Thank you, bright lady, spring-born goddess who opens the doors of life." Pour a libation to her in wine or apple juice. (You may pour it into a bowl and take it outdoors later.) Then drink the rest of the wine or apple juice and eat the apple or share it with friends or animals.

Put your seeds and your jar where you can see them—not in the deep places of the earth, but in the light where you will be reminded of the treasures you kept and that it is now time to plant anew.

Variation if you do not have the seeds you conserved

You will need:
paper and a writing implement
an apple
a glass of white wine or apple juice
a white candle
a burner and incense, preferably patchouli, sandalwood, or myrrh

Optional extras:
an image of Father Dis and Proserpina

Begin by lighting the incense. As you do so, imagine Father Dis as the winter king, an old man with flowing white hair wearing a rich robe of dark cloth, its borders worked with gold thread. He sits on a throne, and about him are all the hidden treasures of the underworld.

Say, "Father Dis, you have kept the seeds of all humanity in your treasury. You have protected it through all of winter's toils. Thank you." The incense is your offering to him. Let it burn for a moment, closing your eyes and imagining the deep, safe places where he holds rulership. "Now it is spring, and I have no seed. Father Dis, please allow me to take some from your deep stores." Imagine standing before his throne, his solemn nod as he gestures to the brimming pots of grain that surround him. He will permit you to fill a bag, and it will be more than enough to sustain you. See yourself filling the bag. Then open your eyes.

Use the paper and writing implement to write down what those seeds are. Maybe they're relationships you've nurtured through the long Winter. Maybe they're skills that you hope to use in the new Spring. Maybe it's a place you've protected, or a person whom you have cared for. Maybe they're ideas that you believe and that you hope will guide the world to come. Write down all the seeds that you hope sprout in this new Spring.

Now address the Queen Proserpina, who sits beside her lord. "Lady—Queen—Proserpina—please return to us with the spring, that these seeds may quicken. Without you, these are simply words. Return to us so that they may be manifest."

Imagine her, golden hair now loose on her shoulders, a circlet of spring flowers on her head. Clad in her white gown, she bids farewell to her husband and king, a parting that is of course temporary, for she will return to him with the turning of the seasons. She carries your jar of seeds in her arms as she turns and walks toward you. Behind her, the Gates of Horn close, shutting away the world below and disappearing. Where her feet touch, flowers spring up, the world greening at her approach.

Say, "Thank you, bright lady." Light the white candle for Proserpina. "Help me plant these seeds. Please grant your blessings so that they will grow and thrive. Golden One, let us be filled with growing sunshine and light, and let the works we undertake be filled with the brightness of spring."

Cut the apple and offer half to Proserpina. "Thank you, bright lady, spring-born goddess who opens the doors of life." Pour a libation to her in wine or apple juice. (You may pour it into a bowl and take it outdoors later.) Then drink the rest of the wine or apple juice and eat the apple or share it with friends or animals.

Put your list where you can see it, where you will be reminded of the treasures that it is now time to plant anew.

Chapter 12

Returning from Battle

Whether we faced an actual war, dispersed civil disturbances, or weathered natural disasters of various kinds, those who defended their communities with force of arms have borne a unique burden. They may have killed other people. They may have watched their friends die. They most certainly have been in situations where they wondered if they would make the ultimate sacrifice—if their lives would be called for to protect others. Warriors face challenges returning from the brink, from that liminal state where they are called to act and to live in ways that others cannot understand.

The Romans recognized that just as there is a time to take up arms, there is also a time to put them down. Then, as now, that wasn't necessarily easy. Therefore, they had a rite specifically designed to help men returning home from war leave behind the things they had seen and done and return to the community and civilian life. This was called the *Armilustrium*, the purification of arms.

When a legion that had been at war returned to Rome, they did not march into the city or have their relatives and friends rush out to greet them. They camped outside the city walls on the Campus Martius, Mars's Field, where the open-air altar to Mars was. They were still wolves, still the guardians who paced the borders, and could not yet enter the city. They camped at least one night out there, and their families were not allowed to see them.

The next day they cleaned their weapons and armor, repaired anything broken or soiled and made it as close as possible to good as new. Their officers and noncommissioned officers reviewed them and they stacked their weapons neatly to be stored away. They received any final pay that was due to them. They packed up their armor and personal possessions, which would be sent to their families separately. Then they entered the city by a special path, wearing only their plain tunics, the long T-shirt–like shirt that fell to above the knee.[58]

There was an alley that led to a neighborhood called Carinae, a narrow alley with two altars on opposite sides of it: one to Juno, the queen of heaven and mother of Mars; the other to Janus, the god of beginnings and endings, of liminal time. Across the alley just below head-height was a thick wooden beam that was anointed with oil, low enough that a man had to stoop to walk beneath it. This was called the *Tigillum*. As he approached the beam, each man was himself anointed and made ritually pure. Then his head was covered with a veil and he walked forward, hopefully stooping in time to creep blindfolded beneath the beam instead of running into it. Once on the other side, he would take off the veil and make a libation at each altar. He had become a citizen again. He was simply a man of the city. Then, and only then, could the waiting wives, children, and parents rush into his arms. They waited on the other side, watching for their loved one to pass underneath and return to them.[59]

A Modern Armilustrium

As we move past the end of the Crisis era, there will be many who fought or served, perhaps on one side or on many sides. One of our tasks as a society will be to help the wolves who have guarded our community, those who have served Mars, return to simply being citizens. How this plays out in terms of public policy is beyond the scope of this book, and the Roman Armilustrium

58. "'Come Mars, God of War'—The Armilustrium," Wunderkammertales, October 19, 2013, https://wunderkammertales.blogspot.com/2015/01/come-mars-god-of-war-armilustrium.html.

59. Livy, *Ab Urbe Condita* (Oxford: Oxford Classical Texts, 1974).

was a formal, civic affair. Nevertheless, we can re-create the ceremonial purification in our groups to help those who have guarded us cross over the threshold and return to civic life. These may be the same people who took part in the Mars ritual earlier, perhaps several years earlier, or they may be different people. This is not, however, a memorial for those who have died. That is an entirely separate rite best done at a different time. This is a liminal rite for the living.

The Armilustrium was celebrated on October 19, which is the best day for it. Another option would be Veterans Day, though if both of these are many months from the time that seems appropriate, choose the first day of the month as the time for beginnings and endings.

This is a community-based ritual. However, if you are alone, you can adapt as needed to your situation.

You will need:

a large wooden beam, like a 2 x 4 (alternatively, a shower curtain rod—directions to follow)

a way to suspend the beam in a doorway (for example, brackets attached to the inside of the doorposts about five feet from the floor)

two altar tables to go in the room beyond the door

a white candle and a blue candle

two goblets of wine and two libation bowls

a dish of sea salt

a dish of honey cakes (you may bake honey cakes or cut store-bought pound cake into small squares and soak with honey)

a vial of oil (preferably carnation or patchouli, though plain olive oil is fine)

two incense burners and incense (one should be rose, violet, or lotus, the other carnation, sandalwood, or myrrh)

something to light candles and incense with

a token, preferably wearable, for each person who is returning (a jacket is perfect. A pin, cap, badge, or patch is also appropriate. The token should be something that can be easily taken off—not a full uniform, for example.)

A white scarf, preferably large and fairly transparent

Optional extras:
a white altar cloth and a blue altar cloth
sprigs of rosemary
bay leaves
an image of Janus
an image of Juno

The people who are to be ritually purified should wait in another room. Ideally this is a quiet place where they can wait thoughtfully, not the kitchen where people are running in and out. If they have loved ones present, they should wait somewhere separately. Yes, they've no doubt seen them since they returned, but they should not see them in the ritual until the proper time. The loved ones should assemble inside the room where the altars will be set up.

For this rite, you need two rooms with a doorway between. In one room, set up the two altars. As you enter, the altar to the left of the door should be to Janus and the altar to the right to Juno. The beam should be attached in the doorway. I've suggested a 2 x 4 cut to size and hung in brackets. If you are not handy, the easiest alternative would be a spring shower curtain rod that can be put at any height and will not mark the door. They come in two sizes, so make sure you get the smaller size that will fit a standard doorway and is meant for a shower stall, not the six-foot one for a bathtub.

Set up the Janus altar with the white altar cloth, the sprigs of rosemary and image of Janus if you are using one, the white candle, a goblet of wine and a libation bowl, an incense burner with carnation, sandalwood, or myrrh, and the dish of sea salt. Also put the vial of oil on this altar.

Set up the Juno altar with the blue cloth, the sprigs of bay and the image of Juno if you are using one, the blue candle, a goblet of wine and a libation bowl, an incense burner with violet, rose, or lotus, and the dish of honey cakes. Also put the white scarf on this altar.

You will need an officiant and an assistant. They may be any experienced people in the group. The assistant's main job is to help loved ones who may not be familiar with the ritual with where to stand and what to do, and to fetch the returning people at the appropriate time.

When everyone has gathered in the room with the altars and the returning people are in another room out of earshot, you may begin.

The Rite

The assistant herds people into a rough semicircle inside the room with the two altars so that they face the door but don't stand directly in front of the altars.

The officiant then speaks a little about the services for the community these returning people have done and explains that this rite is a transition for them to return home. The officiant also explains that this is not a memorial service. This rite is for the living.

OFFICIANT: Hallowed Ones, Janus and Juno, who preside over this rite, please be welcome to our gathering. [Light the white candle for Janus.] Liminal One, lord of beginnings and endings, we ask you to bless those who cross from one role to another, from being our community's keepers, those who walk the boundaries. We thank you for your protection of them, and ask that you hallow their return. [Lights the incense for Janus.] Please bless this oil, that it may serve as a symbol of purification.

Take the oil and open it. Spread it lavishly on the beam that you have placed across the door. This is easier if it's wood and may feel silly if it's a shower curtain rod, but it's the symbol that matters. The assistant may need to help with this and will keep the oil after this is finished.

OFFICIANT: [Go to the Juno altar.] Queen of Heaven, lady of the citadel and of settled places, we ask you to bless those who reenter your society, who return from their guardianship and once again enter into civic life. We thank you for your protection of them and ask that you hallow their return. [Light the incense for Juno and lift the scarf or veil.] Please bless this veil, that it may serve as a symbol of rebirth.

ASSISTANT: [Go to the other room where the returning are waiting.] You have returned, the wolves to their den, the hunter home from the mountains. Come, and lay down your charge and begin anew.

The first returning follows down the hall and stops outside the door with the beam in a place where they can see inside. Each returning does this one at a time, in any order they wish.

ASSISTANT: You have served well, wolf of our people, under the protection of Mars. Are you ready to reenter the City?

RETURNING: I am.

ASSISTANT: Then lay aside your charge, honorably completed.

The returning removes the symbol of their calling—whether it be pin, hat, jacket, or so on—and reverently puts it on a table, chair, or other surface outside the door.

ASSISTANT: Be made new. [Anoint their forehead with the oil.] Be reborn. [Take the veil and put it over their head. It should cover their face but not so much that they can't see to walk. Think bridal veil. It's the same concept.] Enter in.

RETURNING: [Pass under the beam.]

OFFICIANT: [Lift the veil.] Be welcome, Child of the City. Welcome home. [Take the veil off.] The gods have walked with you. Give them your thanks. [Take the returning to the altar of Janus.] You have tasted the salt of your toil, the salt of sweat and blood. [Offer the returning a pinch of the sea salt, which they place on their tongue.] Do you have things you wish to say in the presence of the god?

RETURNING: Janus, thank you for your protection as I walked beyond the boundaries. [You may also speak words of thanksgiving at length in your own words, if you so wish, and then pour a libation to Janus.]

OFFICIANT: So may it be. [Take the returning to the altar of Juno.] Now taste the sweetness of your return, of the love of those who wait for you. [Offer the returning a honey cake, which they eat.] Do you have things you wish to say in the presence of the goddess?

RETURNING: Juno, thank you for the love that greets me as I come home. [You may also speak further in your own words, if you wish, and then pour a libation to Juno.]

OFFICIANT: [To everyone else.] [Name] has returned home! [Loved ones and friends may now crowd in and embrace.]

You may repeat this as many times as necessary to accommodate everyone in the group who is returning and wishes to do this. When everyone has gone, move on to the next bit.

OFFICIANT: Let us all join together in welcoming [names] home!

ASSISTANT: [Quietly remove the beam so that people can leave the room without passing under it.]

It is a good idea to share a meal afterward. This can be a potluck or as elaborate as you wish. Afterward, the libations should be poured outside. The incense can be allowed to burn itself out, and the candles should be extinguished when people are ready to leave the room. Since there was no formal circle-casting, there is no need to have a formal takedown.

Honoring the Dead

Spring may seem a strange time for mourning, but it is necessary to mourn those who have been lost before we can move on, both as a people and as individuals. Mourning in the spring is not actually unusual in our society—Memorial Day, the last Monday in May, is the day that the United States has in the past chosen to honor those who died in service. Traditionally, it has honored veterans of the armed forces, but it is also an appropriate time to mourn those who died for the community, even if they were civilians at the time. The following ritual honors those who have died in the crisis, including both warriors and noncombatants. It may be done either by an individual or by a group as you prefer. It should be done on Memorial Day.

You will need:

a wreath form (wood, plastic, metal, or wicker in any size. An individual will probably want a smaller form and a group a larger one. Wreath forms are readily available at craft stores.)

sturdy tape, like masking tape, packing tape, or florist's tape (or florist's wire if you prefer)

spring flowers and greenery (from your own yard, purchased at a farmer's market, or from anywhere else you like. You may use flowering branches as well if they are ones that bend easily, like azalea.)

a sturdy garden stake

ribbon in colors that coordinate with the flowers

Making the Wreath

Spread out your materials on a table. Take the wreath form and put a little piece of tape on it at the twelve o'clock position. This will be the top of your wreath where you attach the ribbon. Now take a stem of greenery or flower and tape it there so that the stem bends counterclockwise around the wreath. Tape it in at least one more place to keep it secure.

Now take another stem and put it beside the first so that they overlap a little. Secure this stem as well. Begin to work clockwise around the wreath, securing each stem as you go so that each new piece overlaps the stems of the previous pieces, hiding the tape. All the stems should be going in the same direction, each one with the flower or greenery counterclockwise of the stem. Fill in so that the wreath form beneath it is not visible.

When you have gone all the way around, you will have a floral wreath. Add or subtract here and there to make it look balanced. Then make a bow with the ribbon and attach it at the top so that the long ends of the ribbon fall down over the hole in the center of the wreath.

Attach the garden stake to the back so that you have a way to stake the wreath to the ground. (If you prefer an actual wreath stand—a tripod that holds a wreath—these are often available at craft stores.)

A Wreath-Laying

Once you have made the wreath, you will formally lay it to honor the dead. This is an old practice that has gone out of fashion. Through much of the twentieth century, various organizations and societies laid wreaths at the graves of various people to honor them, most popularly at veterans' memorials on Memorial Day or Veterans Day. Sometimes these ceremonies were very complex and formal, such as the observances at the Tomb of the Unknown Soldier at Arlington National Cemetery. Other times they were fairly simple, like a group of Girl Scouts laying a wreath at the grave of Juliette Gordon Low, the founder of the Girl Scouts. It might be done by a group of citizens on the anniversary of a shipwreck or natural disaster. Recently, the formal wreath-laying has been superseded by the spontaneous outpourings of flowers and teddy bears at the scene of a recent disaster or shooting. Those, however, are usually immediately after the event. A wreath-laying commemorates those who died in the years and decades after their passing, not just in the immediate aftermath.

Think about who you would like to honor in this way. It may be a national leader, or it may be a loved one personally known to you who died in the recent cataclysm. It may be a group of people, like the veterans' section of a cemetery or even a mass grave. It may be at the site of a disaster rather than at a grave, like at the annual observance of September 11 where there is a wreath-laying at the memorial in the field in Pennsylvania where Flight 93 crashed as the passengers struggled against their hijackers.

However, be aware that even if you choose to honor a loved one known to you, your choice is political. If your loved one was on "the wrong side," the side that didn't win, honoring them in any way may be seen as an act of defiance or a reactionary statement. One of the first things that winners in most conflicts do is stigmatize or criminalize memorialization of the other side. Reconciliation requires everyone being able to mourn people they loved, but depending on how the crisis has ended, reconciliation may not be at the top of anyone's agenda. If you find that laying a wreath publicly at a grave or other site is too dangerous for you, it is completely appropriate to perform this rite at home in front of a picture or symbol of those you mourn.

Alternately, if you are on "the right side," please understand and show compassion for those who have lost loved ones and need to mourn them, even if you did not agree politically with their loved ones in life. There used to be a saying, "Every soldier is someone's son." Or wife, or husband, or parent, or lover, or sibling. Remember that saying if you are the winner. Allowing people to express grief is a gesture of basic humanity.

The Rite

Take your wreath to the site you have chosen. If it is a public place, like a cemetery or memorial, you may find it easy to do this. If it's a private site, like a school or hospital, you may have to lay your wreath outside the boundaries.

Holding your offering, speak aloud who you are dedicating this to and why. You may be as long or short as you wish. You may explain what they did that was worthy and good, or simply express your grief at a life cut short. You may recite or read something important to them—for example, Dr. King's words at his memorial, or The American's Creed at some veterans' cemeteries. You may, alone or with others, sing something appropriate to the occasion, whether the music is religious or secular (some Memorial Day observances include a bugler playing "Taps"). Remember them.

Once you have done these things, place the wreath with dignity and grace. If you have a stake or tripod, fix it firmly in the ground so that the wreath will not tip over. Then back away from it, not turning your back on your tribute until you are some distance away in order to show respect. (If you are in a cemetery, try not to walk on other graves as you do this, as that is disrespectful. Walk on the aisles between the graves.)

Observing the dead with solemn respect is an important part of ending the era of Winter.

The End of Winter

Winter has come to an end. Perhaps with fanfare, or perhaps as imperceptibly and gradually as swelling buds on trees signal the end of seasonal winter. What do you feel? Relief? Joy? Grief? Or perhaps just utter exhaustion. You have survived the great cataclysm of your time.

What will you do with the rest of your life?

Step forward with me into Spring.

Chapter 13

After Long Winter

Two Thousand Years Ago

It is just before dawn on a beautiful day at the beginning of summer. Although it's early, and the stars are still bright above, the sky has begun to pale in the east, and the procession moving through the streets needs the illumination of the torches in their iron cressets. There must be fifty people, but they walk silently, as though at a funeral. The man in the midst of the procession wears the folds of his toga over his head like a hood just as a mourner, or perhaps a penitent, would. The procession makes its way slowly through the twisting streets of Rome, some streets overhung by *insulae*—apartment buildings four or five stories tall with shops on the ground floors. A few people watch from the windows, and a street sweeper pauses on a cobbled side street to watch the procession pass. They use no litters, but go on foot, their treads marking out the paths of the city.

The sky lightens to a shell pink on the horizon when they reach the high altar on the hill. The breeze freshens, torches streaming in the air. There is more of a crowd here, including a choir of boys and girls, whispering and pushing each other nervously until their director tells them to be quiet. There are priests as well, bringing platters of twenty-seven cakes, nine each of three kinds. There is no blood sacrifice today. This is a day to forgive blood. Instead, the offering is cake.

The man at the center of the procession steps forward, baring his head to the lightening sky. He's young, no more than 35, with a square jaw and wavy brown hair. He is Marcus Vipsanius Agrippa, the husband of Julia—the only child of the Emperor Augustus—and the emperor's best friend. He is the greatest general of his generation—the man who defeated Marc Antony at Actium and Alexandria, who conquered Egypt for Augustus and ended the Roman Civil War. A few years ago he celebrated Augustus's Triumph, Antony's and Cleopatra's children walking in chains through the streets of Rome. He is either a great hero or a great villain, depending on one's point of view.

For decades civil war had convulsed Rome. Battles had fallen out as literally brother against brother: members of the same family backing Caesar or Pompey, Caesar's assassins or Caesar's avengers, Augustus or Antony. Casualties from each battle numbered in the thousands, and battle followed battle for years. Augustus finally triumphed not ten years before this morning, and Agrippa won the battles that made his victory so. But this morning he is not here to make war. This morning, he is here to make peace.

He lifts the first offering plate, looking out across the expectant crowd. The children's choir stills as a gray-haired man steps up, the poet and composer of the day's rites. His voice carries, the voice of a man used to speaking in public and commanding audiences. "Oh Phoebus, Oh Diana Queen of the Woodlands, bright heavenly glories now worshiped and cherished forever, now grant what we pray for at this sacred time!"

Agrippa places the plate on the altar just as the rising sun lifts clear of the horizon, Apollo's bright chariot climbing the heavens, sunlight striking the top of the hill, the men, the choir, and the white altar. A saeculum has ended by night. Another began with the dawn.

Invoking Concordia in Rome

These events are true and part of the historical record, occurring in 17 BCE early in the reign of the Emperor Augustus. We know who participated, where the rites were held, what the sacrifices were, and even parts of the ritual itself. The procession began at the Temple of Concordia and, after the offerings this morning, returned there in celebration as part of a three-day festival called the Saecular Games, the official beginning to a new saeculum. Theater performances and athletic contests were held as well as six rites. The rite described here was the penultimate rite.

How do you end a civil war? How do you end a period beginning with "let loose the dogs of war?"[60] How do you bring people back together into a society that is not constantly struggling against itself? A few years after the defeat of Antony, the lasting rifts must have been apparent. Was there any chance that this peace was more than an interlude before another round of war began?

A conscious decision was made to seek reconciliation instead of revenge, to ritualize peacemaking. This is not to say that Augustus was a good man, or that he had any other motive than the selfish one of securing his throne, but he clearly recognized that if the government and individual citizens continued to seek revenge, restitution, or even justice for all the acts that had been committed during the decades of internal war, Rome would simply collapse. The state would dissolve into warring provinces again, held by one senator or contender against the others, just as it had for the last twenty-five years. There would be no lasting peace as long as any group claimed grievances against another and acted upon them.

This is a strange notion to our modern eyes. We are certain that peace results from justice, and that unless all guilty parties are punished there can be no reconciliation. But what do you do if all parties are guilty? What do you do if there has been so much bloodshed, so much persecution, so much tit for tat, that to punish the guilty would be to punish nearly everyone? You can't jail the whole society. You can't put on trial 50 percent of the population. You can't punish by deprivation or loss of income and freedom most of a society unless you simply reduce the entire society to poverty and a fringe existence. That's happened before. History teaches us this always goes badly because it results in another round of grievances, in the anger of children who grow up deprived because of the sins of their ancestors and who want

---

60. William Shakespeare, *Julius Caesar* (New York: Simon & Schuster, 2004).

to get back at those whom they now perceive as oppressors. And it results in the triumphant party carrying punishment out too far, becoming the oppressors they once denounced. An examination of the revolutions of the last two centuries provides myriad examples of this. This was also what was happening in Rome.

Augustus and Agrippa understood that if they were to build a stable state, they needed to not only defeat Antony's party, but also to reconcile Romans to one another and to at least outwardly restore civility and the rule of law. Toward this end in 17 BCE, they revived the ancient festival of the Saecular Games, last celebrated in 146 BCE. There were six main rites over three nights and three days. The nighttime rites were respectively dedicated to the Fates, to the *Ilythiae* (goddesses of childbirth), and to Terra Mater (Mother Earth), and were rites of penance and propitiation. The daytime rites, in contrast, were invocations, asking Jupiter, Juno, and Apollo and Diana to favor the Roman state and to return prosperity and peace.[61]

Propitiation, penance, punishment—at this point, it's necessary to examine the difference between these ideas. Punishment is most straightforward: to hurt someone in retribution for something they have done, said, thought, or supported. This can be physical punishment, like whipping or confinement, or the removal of rights and privileges like voting, attending school or public meetings, or speaking in public. It can be social punishment, like shunning or shaming or forcing people to wear humiliating clothing or insignias. Punishment is imposed on people by other people. It is not consensual.

Penance is entirely consensual. Penance is a self-imposed limitation that a person chooses to make up for something they have done, said, or thought. It may be physical, like fasting or self-flagellation, or it may be social, like engaging in community service or denying oneself companionship, sex, or pleasure. Penance is restitution or self-denial: paying for the car you wrecked, speaking out for the people you harmed, or giving up using Twitter if you harmed someone there. Penance is personal and internal and cannot be done to someone else.

---

61. Inscription found in Rome at the Tarentum, dating from 17 BCE.

Propitiation is more complex. Propitiation assumes that an individual's actions are part of a larger pattern—part of the work of the Furies, as the Greeks would have said: part of a frenzy of activities, a wild moment. For example, in wars, people do things they would not ordinarily do. Mobs and riots take actions that the individuals wouldn't have undertaken alone. Crimes are committed, people are hurt, and terrible things happen in this frenzy. Later, individuals may wonder how: How could we have been part of that? How could we have thought that was okay? Who are we to have done that? In the Classical world, there was a phrase for this: "The Furies possessed us." Eris, Discordia, and the Furies walked in human form within us. Therefore, the deities who have been offended, those who have been misused, must be apologized to.

It is interesting which deities Augustus and Agrippa decided to propitiate, to apologize to for the Roman Civil Wars, and to beg forgiveness from going forward. First, the Fates, the *Moerae*, received their sacrifice on the night of May 31. If this had simply been the fate of so many to perish, surely the Fates could be kinder! If it was simply time for social upheaval, for the end of the saeculum, then now it was time to turn the wheel forward and let the Fates spin a new thread.

The Ilythiae, the goddesses of childbirth and of children unborn, received their sacrifice on the next night. This is the most obscure and difficult of the choices—was this for so many children and mothers killed during the wars? For the children who would never be born because of so many premature deaths? For the Ilythiae in their chthonic role as guides who bring children out of the underworld and into our world at birth? Virgil's *Aeneid*, a work contemporary to this festival and associated with both Augustus and Agrippa, shows the souls of children yet to be born dwelling in the underworld just as the souls of the dead do, awaiting the moment when the Gates of Ivory open above them, and they rise into the light as though traversing a birth canal. Perhaps the apology was intended for those children who were never given life and who waited in vain.

Lastly, on the night of June 2, sacrifices were made to Mother Earth. She and all her works—animals and plants, fields and waters—had borne the damage of war. Propitiation was offered for orchards burned, horses slain in battle, forests destroyed, rivers running with blood. Mother Earth herself had been offended by the slaughter, and apologies to her had to be rendered by the Emperor Augustus himself.

Once the offended deities had been appeased and discord abjured, healing could begin. The three daytime ceremonies were designed to invoke the deities who fed concord rather than discord and to invite them to once again rule over the Roman state and restore peace, prosperity, and happiness.

On June 1, the morning after the first propitiation, the invocation was to *Jupiter Optimus Maximus*, Jupiter Most High. As the king of the gods, he was the patron of good governance, of the well-run state operating within the rule of law for the benefit of its citizens. Strong of arm, he did not need to resort to war to achieve his aims but could simply exert authority—*auctoritas*, the power of correct action. Under auctoritas, individuals and nations act rationally to do the right thing, bringing to bear what we now call "soft power." Rome triumphs with roads and theaters, markets and trade ships, language and culture, as well as with the power of her legions.

The second invocation was to Juno Regina—queen of the heavens, wife, mother, and divine protector. She is bountiful, the giver of riches. Grain barges, workshops brimming with pottery and cloth, gold, and honey flowing in inexhaustible wealth belong to her. She is plenty. Even the poor have enough to eat, and all the people can rejoice in her riches. Life just keeps getting better as a rising tide lifts all boats. There is enough for everyone.

Lastly, the final invocation was to the twins, Apollo and Diana. We know exactly what was said because it was written by the poet Horace and survives to this day.

> Gentle and peaceful Apollo, lay down your arms,
> And listen now to the young lads' supplications:
> Luna, crescent-horned queen of the constellations,
> Give ear to the girls ...
> Then, you divinities, show our receptive youth
> Virtue, grant peace and quiet to the old, and give

Children and wealth to the people of Romulus,
And every glory ...
Now Faith and Peace, Honor, and ancient Modesty,
Dare to return once more, with neglected Virtue,
And blessed Plenty dares to appear again, now,
With her flowing horn.
May Phoebus, the augur, decked with the shining bow,
Phoebus who's dear to the Nine Muses, that Phoebus
Who can offer relief to a weary body
With his healing art,
May he, if he favors the Palatine altars,
Extend Rome's power, and Latium's good-fortune,
Through the fresh ages, show, always, improvement.[62]

They prayed that the old may have peace, quiet, and good health, that the young may have virtue and glory, and that all may have honor, plenty, faith, and dignity. It ended with this: "May we always show improvement." What a prayer for the state! May we always show improvement! May we continue to be a better people and a better nation.

In the decades after this great civic rite, Rome reached an unimagined apex of power—*Pax Romana*, Roman Peace, an empire extending from Britain to Sudan. While scandals and tragedies beset the imperial family—bad emperors squandering wealth and good emperors building it—for the most part, it was an era of peace and prosperity. As the decades turned, of course new injustices grew beneath the surface and old ones festered, but for many people within the empire it was an era of unprecedented mobility and civilization. Augustus and Agrippa achieved what they meant to do with this rite, the Saecular Games. They ushered in a new era that outlasted their lifetimes.

---

62. Horace, *Carmen Seculare*, trans. A. S. Kline (London: Poetry in Translation, 2005).

Invoking Concordia in More Modern Times

Eighteen hundred years later, another people deliberately invoked Concordia for exactly the same reasons.

Visiting Paris today, La Place de la Concorde is a beautiful square in the midst of the city, with elaborate nineteenth-century fountains and an obelisk given to France by Egypt as a symbol of friendship. It's a lovely place. It's hard to imagine that a little more than two hundred years ago it was the site of 1,119 cruel killings.[63] Men and women were executed in this square, their heads chopped off by the guillotine, including the former king and queen, Louis XVI and Marie Antoinette.

The French Revolution began in 1789 as the result of decades of widening disconnection between the elites and the people. Wealthy aristocrats wielded greater and greater economic power, while more and more people at the bottom fell into poverty. Efforts to change things, to ameliorate poverty and to modernize law and economy, were stalled or halted by the elites. King Louis XV's attitude was key: "Après moi le deluge." After me, the flood. After me, chaos. Who cares what happens after I'm dead?

Unaddressed problems grew worse until they reached a breaking point. While the Revolution began as an attempt to force the king to accept a constitutional monarchy constrained by the rule of the Estates General, once the floodgates were opened, the flood could not be contained. Between 1792 and 1794, more than one hundred fifty thousand French citizens were killed either in the Terror or in fighting between various factions and rebel groups, not counting the forty thousand or more soldiers killed either in internal fighting or in the war with Austria. Everyone with a grudge to settle settled it, neighbors denouncing neighbors guilty of wrong thinking, of wrong sympathies, or even of not being sufficiently enthusiastic about revolutionary ideas. An accusation was enough to send people, and perhaps their families, to the guillotine. We have the idea today that only aristocrats were denounced and killed, but most of the victims of the Terror were not

---

63. "25 Avril 1792: Première Utilisation de la Guillotine sur un Condamné," France-pittoresque
.com, April 25, 2019, https://www.france-pittoresque.com/spip.php?article5744.

wealthy—merely people who drew the wrath of the mob. As each group of revolutionaries was denounced by the next faction, those who followed the previous ideology were imprisoned or killed.

For a little more than two years anyone and everyone was in danger, and thousands of people denounced people they disliked—an annoying neighbor, a mother-in-law whose property was attractive, a boss who had been unsympathetic, or simply a stranger who held different opinions. Tens of thousands of people were part of the mob, the denouncers, those who cheered at the foot of the guillotine, and tens of thousands feared for their lives in this constantly moving coil of ideologies and opinions. Today's correct words were tomorrow's horrible offense. How could a person know what to say or do? How could anyone avoid being the target of everyone's grievance? Any person who had ever disliked you could turn you in.

How does a society come back from that? How do you walk away from the bodies and other atrocities and get back to any kind of functional society when your former employee killed your son and your wife's disgruntled former brother-in-law caused her to be imprisoned and abused? When you, yourself, are responsible for the death of the person who argued rudely with you and whom the mob literally tore apart? When your sister denounced the man whose shop she used to work in and caused the death of his entire family? How do you stop?

In October 1795, a new government was formed, the Directory, which hoped to somehow leash these Furies. The executions stopped and the guillotine was removed, but that was simply the beginning. How could France heal? What do you do when *everyone* is perpetrator or victim, and many people are both? The process of forging a new national identity that sought to bring together all French would be a lengthy one, and would certainly not be accomplished swiftly or without lasting scars, but one of the first steps had to be the symbolic cleansing and reconsecration of civil spaces. After all, a large public square in the middle of the capital city can't be ignored! There it is. Everyone knows what happened there. The space first known as Place Louis XV under the king and then Place de la Revolution under the guillotine had to be addressed.

The Directors were mindful of symbolism and sought to use it wisely. Therefore, before the end of 1795, the square was physically cleaned of all traces of the guillotine and renamed in a public ceremony invoking the Classical principle of Concordia. As Place de la Concorde, it was a focus of renewed civil authority, of the idea of the rule of law bringing just order rather than discordian Liberty with her Phrygian cap and bloody hands. Tamed, Liberty became a just goddess, a guardian of public virtue and the Rights of Man. Concordia reigned.

Why We Need Concordia: Action vs. Identity

One of the keys to concord is the question of action vs. identity. What is the difference between the phrases "you have committed a crime" and "you are a criminal"? The first is an action, a thing that a person chose to do, and they may in the future choose to do otherwise. The second is an identity, which in our society is an unchosen, irreducible fundamental of personality. Our society has taught us that you can't change your identity. You are born with it, and it is who you are. If you appear to change, it's merely revelation—you were always really X, and you have only now discovered it or revealed it to the world. If you are a criminal, it is simply your destiny to commit criminal acts. There is no rehabilitation because there is no choice. You cannot choose to be other than your identity.

This is a model the left has embraced because in many ways it made the debate easier on issues like sexual orientation. This model breaks down completely on other issues, like minority religious identity. After all, don't we have a choice about which religion we practice? We choose to do something nonmainstream when we practice Paganism. The only way to claim we don't choose—and of course some see it this way—is to say that we are in a cult and lack the free will to decide what we believe. We must argue that there is absolutely nothing wrong with our nonmainstream choice. It's not biological. It's not a cult. We are choosing to do something because we want to and we think it's right and it harms no one in society if we do so. We have to make a positive argument for what we believe, rather than argue that we can't help it.

Of course there are people who say, "I've always been different, and I've always known I belonged to the Old Gods even before I knew what that meant." And there are others who say, "I never heard of any of this until I was forty, but it makes so much sense!" Both of them are right. Both of these are valid experiences. We defend our beliefs and our identity, whether they were heartfelt from infancy or suddenly discovered decades later. In other words, it doesn't matter why someone is Pagan. It doesn't matter whether they came in desperation, in love, or simply because somebody invited them to a party. They all belong. If you choose to be here, here you are. You are a Pagan if you do Pagan stuff. Needless to say, a person can stop doing Pagan stuff and stop identifying as Pagan anytime. Nobody is going to go after them and bring them back or judge them because they once went to a ritual and then decided it wasn't for them.

But that's not how the mainstream in our society sees things. Identity is growing more and more codified, and as it does, identity depends less and less on actions that you choose to take—or rather, an action defines identity forever.

What is the difference between "you have committed a crime" and "you are a criminal"? A criminal has no choice. They simply are a criminal, and there is no way they can stop being a criminal. They have no free will. When it's phrased as "you have committed a crime," the equation changes. Think about these:

- "You drank too much and wrecked your car." "You are a drunk."
- "You teased a classmate and made him cry." "You are a bully."
- "You said something offensive to a coworker." "You are a sexual harasser."
- "You stole something." "You are a thief."

An action can be undone or atoned for, broken things restored, restitution given. An action can be put in the past, unlike an identity, which is forever. An action can be regretted and not repeated. An identity can only be embraced. An apology can be rendered and accepted. A person can say, "I'm sorry I said this thing. I won't do it again," and then go on with life, rather than being shunned forever.

This is critical when many, *many* people have committed the offense. Imagine, for example, that every person you know who had been part of an online shaming mob was called to account. Imagine if every participant had to embrace the identity "online bully" in every social space for the rest of their lives. Imagine if every person they met, every potential client or employer, every future son-in-law, every grandchild, had to understand why they were a terrible person. What would result from that? Identity is immutable. Online Bully is their new name.

Would that solve problems or would that create more? If enough people are being punished together, don't they instead deny the crime and fight back? Don't they especially do so when the punishment begins to outweigh the original offense in terms of severity?

Viewing offenses as actions rather than identities does not excuse the actions. However, it allows them to be atoned for. Restitution is possible. And then it's over. Punishing identity rather than action only leads to another cycle. In a situation like the French Revolution, where many people had both committed terrible acts and been victims of terrible acts, identity as perpetrator or victim could not offer a way forward. Only concord and reconciliation could offer any hope of coming out of this as a nation.

Journaling Exercise

For this journaling exercise, you will need a notebook, a journal, or an electronic means of writing. You will also need a quiet space and some uninterrupted time.

Think about a time you were punished in what you feel was an out-of-proportion response to what you did. It may be something that happened when you were a child—you lost a toy for a week for being a smart-mouth—or it may be something much more serious, like serving jail time for possession of a small amount of marijuana. How did you feel about it? Were you repentant or angry? How do you feel about it today?

Think about something you did in the past that you truly regret, whether or not you were punished for it. Maybe it's hurtful words to a lover that led to a breakup, or maybe it's something more serious—a moment of carelessness that caused a car accident that killed someone. How does your regret change you? What have you done differently because of your regret?

Do you believe in second chances? Do you believe a person can change? Or do you believe that once someone has shown their true colors, no change is possible?

Think about a time you have forgiven someone. What had they done? Why did you forgive them? What happened after that?

Do you believe that people are responsible for the crimes of others in a group they belong to, whether that group is religious, ethnic, racial, political, or otherwise? Do you believe that the children of perpetrators are tainted by their parents' crimes? Do those children or other members of the group owe restitution? Or do you believe that only the perpetrators of the crime should be punished?

These are not easy questions, and you may need to take some time to think about each one. How we answer these questions as individuals and as a society will shape how we interact with each other and what we are able to build in the next saeculum.

We can know, however, that Concordia will be necessary to bring us into the new era. She will be critical to help us reconcile, just as she was in the wake of the Roman wars of the triumvirates and as she was in the wake of the French Revolution.

Reconciliation is often done by the creation or reconsecration of public spaces and by large civil rites that are designed to bring people back together. Look for these kinds of activities as positive indicators that change is coming based on inclusion rather than exclusion, on consent rather than force. If the activities are well designed, they will celebrate coming together rather than the defeat of any person, ideology, or people. Celebrations of defeat continue grievances into the next saeculum, whereas reconciliations create lasting concord.

There is a difference between celebrations of victory and celebrations of defeat. Contrast Augustus's Triumph with the young children of his dead enemies walking through the streets in chains, with the celebrations in New York at the end of World War II, where Axis symbols, prisoners, captives, or loot were completely absent. No German or Japanese prisoners of war were paraded through the streets in chains in the United States. Victory and vengeance do not go hand in hand. There are choices about how to win, and we must make them deliberately.

Welcoming Concordia

While large civic rituals are beyond the scope of this book, we can each welcome Concordia quietly into our own lives. Now that we've thought about our hopes for (and fears of) the aftermath, the next rite will help us invoke Concordia as we enter the next phase.

You will need:
a white candle
a means to light it
your previous journal entries or notes

The Rite

Find a quiet place where you will not be interrupted. Light the candle. Say, "Concordia, we stand at the turning. The world is changed. My life is changed. We set a new course. Help us to reach for you. Help us to seek your reconciliation between individuals and peoples. Help us to end the war of all against all and find respite and hope again."

You may wish to add those with whom you hope to become reconciled. Perhaps you have loved ones who have been on a different path. Perhaps you have lost people you hope to find. Perhaps you simply wish that parts of your life could be less dominated by conflicts. Say aloud those hopes. Express them positively. Say, "I would like to find common ground with my in-laws and be able to be a family again," rather than "I would like my in-laws to see that I was right." This is not about winning. This is about peace. Your notes can help you think through what you want to say and how you want to say it.

Then offer your hopes for healing. Say, "Concordia, help us heal the wounds we have taken, as individuals and as a society. Help us begin to heal." You may find this very emotional if your experiences are raw. Remember, you are not asking for healing to be complete. It may not be for many years. You are asking for her aid to begin the process.

When you have expressed yourself to Concordia, thank her for listening and blow the candle out.

You are ready to move into the next phase. It's time to think about how to heal the world in the aftermath of the fire.

..... Chapter 14 .....

Peace

Würzburg, Germany, 1946

The house has a roof, its brick and half-timbering neatly repaired. The boy doesn't need to see the American flag flying outside to know this is the home of an American senior officer. There's a roof, and there aren't many houses in Würzburg with roofs right now. He stands hesitating, a skinny blond boy in ragged clothes, a half-grown boxer puppy next to him on a leash that's just a piece of string. But she's a good dog and she sits neatly at heel, not pulling on the string at all. He takes a deep breath, filling out his chest, and then knocks on the door.

A woman answers, an expression of surprise crossing her face as she looks down at him. She's in her forties, brown hair pinned up over hazel-green eyes and a face creased from smiling. "Yes?" she says in German with a terrible accent.

He swallows. "I heard you buy things," he says. "Women say so. They say you buy things they make. Bracelets out of copper wire, out of cartridges, carvings out of wood, things they salvage." Würzburg has been half-destroyed by bombs. There's a word for the scavengers: *trümmerfrau*, rubble women. They make things out of what they find. This woman buys them, more copper bracelets than anyone could ever need, more little figures carved from a house beam.

She looks like she didn't understand everything he said. Her German's not good. But she got the sense of it. "I buy things," she says. "You sell?" She holds out her hand as though ready to see what he has, no doubt expecting some little ornament that's worth a meal or two, something better than what they give out at the Displaced Persons Camp.

He swallows. He pulls on the leash. "This is Asta," he says. "My parents..." He stops but makes himself go on. "We bred dogs in Saxony. Good dogs, fine dogs for boar hunting. They..." He does stop now. Asta stands up, her front feet on his legs, licking his face as though she understands every word he says. After all, she lost her family too. He doesn't look at the woman, just rubs Asta's ears. "She is the last puppy. I don't have her papers. I just have her. We got away together. She was so tiny I carried her in my shirt. I walked and walked. I fed her. I kept her warm. And we are here now."

"You're at the DP camp?" The woman's eyes are bright.

"They say I can't keep her. There is no room for dogs. So I sleep outside and I feed her half my food." He swallows. "But it's not enough. She's so thin. It's stunting her growth. Asta needs food." He straightens up and looks her in the eyes, like his father always told him a man should. "Frau Colonel, I hear you are a nice woman who likes dogs. I would like to sell Asta to you. She is the last of a great breed. She will be a good dog for you."

The woman bends down, holding her hand out to Asta, letting Asta smell her. Then she pets her, gently but with the firmness of someone who knows dogs, who isn't afraid of big hunting dogs, though Asta doesn't have the weight of her breed yet and might never. She pets Asta thoughtfully, like she's figuring something out.

"She's worth some money," he says. He swallows. Asta is beyond price.

"Yes." She stands up. "I'll buy Asta. But you see I don't really have much time for a dog. I'm going to have to hire a boy to take care of her for me. He'll need to take her for walks three times a day and feed her at dinnertime. So it would have to be a very responsible boy who could come and take care of her for me." She looks at him very seriously. "I suppose I could hire you, if you weren't too busy."

"Hire me to take care of Asta?" He can hardly believe his ears.

"I'll pay you to walk her, of course," the woman says. She holds out her hand. "Do we have a deal?"

Every day. He will see Asta every day. He'll take care of her. "Yes," he says, and clasps her hand. A thought strikes him. "Don't you have a boy of your own?"

"My boy is older than you," she says, and there is a lightness in her voice that doesn't touch her eyes. "He's at home with my sister getting well. He was shelled on the Rhine Crossing and had to have another operation on his hand."

He goes cold. Her son was hurt by them, and who knows who was hurt by her son?

And yet he is still holding her hand, Asta sniffing at her knees hopefully.

"I think we can take good care of Asta together," she says gently. "Don't you?"

"Yes," he says. "I do."

1978

The girl is about 10, perching on a stool beside the olive Naugahyde recliner that the old man lies in. "And what happened then?" she demands. "What happened to Asta and what happened to the boy?"

Retired Colonel Edwards is very gaunt, nearly 90 years old, and this is his step-grandchild. "The boy lived in the camp and walked Asta every day for a year. And then the Red Cross found an aunt of his who had refugeed to Bremen and was safe. The poor woman had been looking frantically for him and had almost given up. So he went to live with his aunt in Bremen. Asta stayed with us and we brought her back to the States with us. We bred her several times and she had the most beautiful puppies. She's a founding mother of a line around here. She lived almost until you were born, and her grandpuppies are around today. She was the best dog ever, a real good girl, and your granny loved her so much."

The little girl's eyes are shining. "Where'd granny get the idea of having him take care of her?"

"I reckon it was the Book of Exodus."

She digests this a minute, and then she asks delicately, "So why didn't you hate him? Why didn't she hate him? I mean, they'd just shot Daddy."

The old man looks off into space, like he's seeing something far from this comfortable paneled den. "I fought the Germans in the Great War when I was a young man. I fought them again when I was middle-aged. I never want to do it again. I never want us to go to war like that again, kin on kin, and we didn't. We didn't fight Germany again in 1970, and that's the real victory. My best war, Angel, is the one we never had to fight. There's something more important than being a good loser. It's being a good winner. Don't you forget that. Remember it when it's your war."

"I will," she promises.

———— • ————

My granny, the same young woman who was hosting the séance in chapter 2, was faced with a question she'd never imagined: How do you treat people who just shot your child? How do you take care of people who just killed millions in concentration camps? How do you, personally, behave to women whose sons or husbands committed unspeakable atrocities, while your son who is all of 22 is still having multiple surgeries to correct a wound that may never heal entirely?

You're the winner. You have all the power. You can punish. You can take revenge. You can even call it righteousness.

Instead, my granny was kind. Instead, she helped a refugee boy and his dog. She bought handicrafts by the bushel to put money into the hands of refugee women, helped the Red Cross find relatives for unaccompanied children, helped people find housing and lost family members, and was polite to the veterans who began to be repatriated. "I treated them the way I would want Bunky treated," she said. She treated the sons of her enemies the way she wanted her son treated, not asking whether they deserved it, not asking whether they were guilty.

Could we do as much? That's the question I have asked myself since 1978. That's the question I've asked since my step-grandfather first told me this story. If I were in my granny's shoes, could I be the hands of the Mother of the World? I ask myself now, if someone had shot my daughter, could I be kind to their kin? Would I avenge myself on their children and call it justice?

I like to think that I would not. I would try not to. I have asked myself this hard question for a long time, and I have my granny's example to follow. I would try to live my values. I hope I would succeed.

A Question for the Community

But this was not merely a question for individuals. At the end of the last Crisis era, World War II, we had choices. The Secretary of the Treasury, Henry Morgenthau Jr., put forth a plan in 1944 that proposed what would happen after the Allied defeat of Germany. The Morgenthau Plan, as it was named, proposed among other things that Germany should be partitioned and should never again be a single state, that the Ruhr industrial area should be deindustrialized by the destruction of all manufacturing capability and that Ruhr's population should be forcibly removed to other areas except for a small number of farmers who would not be allowed to mine or produce anything else, and that restitution for the war should be accomplished in part by "forced German labor outside Germany."[64]

Imagine for a moment what the world would now look like if this plan had been enacted. Imagine what the United States would have become.

The Morgenthau Plan was not adopted, and it's now an obscure historical footnote. Instead, the Marshall Plan was enacted. Put forward by the new Secretary of State, retired General George Marshall, the Marshall Plan stated that "an orderly and prosperous Europe requires the economic contributions of a stable and productive Germany."[65] Instead of vengeance, the United States launched a massive humanitarian effort to relieve refugee and human suffering in Germany and to rehabilitate German infrastructure and industry. Individuals guilty of war crimes were tried for those crimes, but the population of Germany as a whole was not punished. Nor were future generations to be

---

64. Henry Morgenthau Jr., "Suggested Post-Surrender Program for Germany," preserved at the Franklin D. Roosevelt Presidential Library and Museum, September, 1944.

65. "The Marshall Plan," *Time* 50, no. 4 (July 28, 1947), http://content.time.com/time /magazine/0,9263,7601470728,00.html.

penalized for the acts of their ancestors through denial of education, travel, resources, or the right to vote. No one was transported abroad to forced labor—or, to give it its proper name, slavery. Instead of revenge, we sought reconciliation.

The success of that approach is readily apparent. For seventy years, Germany has been one of our staunchest allies in Europe. We have benefited immensely, as have they, from decades of friendship.

This plan was put into effect by people like my step-grandfather, Colonel Raymond Edwards, and my grandmother, the young woman who held the séance back in the second chapter. As young people, the Lost Generation dreamed of making an impossible difference. As middle-aged people, their choice was how to live their values in a Crisis era, whether as governors of refugee camps or as a woman who helped a boy and a dog.

Being a good winner is hard. Putting aside revenge and reaching for concord is hard, but as we reach the last phase of Winter, these are the discussions we must have. No longer solely focused on surviving the crisis, we must consider what we want the resolutions of the crisis to be. While we look forward to the resolution of the next Crisis era, we would do well to remember the resolution of the last one. We chose Concordia, and the positive impacts of that choice echoed to every part of the world for generations. It is not yet clear what the exact parameters of our future choices will be, but you will have a voice in what we choose with your words and your actions. May we act with compassion in victory, and may Concordia rule our interactions so that the world to come is the best we can make it.

A Rite to Invoke Concordia

In Roman religion, Concordia is the daughter of Mars and Venus. That's the context for this rite. While great civic rites involving tens of thousands are beyond the scope of this book, this rite is designed for a local group, such as an Outer Temple or UU congregation, who is seeking a new beginning based on peace and reconciliation.

To create sacred space, you will need two experienced officiants to play the roles of Mars and Venus and two more people of any experience level to play the roles of Mercury and Iris (this rite is less participatory and therefore allows completely inexperienced people to take part). This rite takes the form of a "tableau," an instructive play that was a feature of Classical religion. This is suited to a group, and if you are alone you may modify it as you need to.

You will need:

a space large enough for everyone to gather comfortably. If you have people who will need to sit, it is fine to offer chairs. If you have children attending, they can sit on the floor in front if they like.

an altar set up at one end of the space (make sure there's enough room around the altar and gathering areas for someone to comfortably walk around them)

the most beautiful image of a baby that you can find (whether this is stone, resin, ceramic, or even a plastic baby doll. It should be wrapped in a white baby blanket and nestled into a large basket as though it were a real sleeping newborn.)

a large white candle

a red candle

a blue candle

a libation goblet full of wine

a libation bowl

a large basket or dish for offerings

an incense holder and incense (sandalwood, laurel, and myrrh are all appropriate)

something to light candles and incense

a sword for Mars

appropriate clothing for Venus and Mars. You may go two ways with this: you may opt for Classical robing, with Mars wearing a red tunic (with or without armor and helmet) and appropriate Classical accessories and with Venus wearing a flowing blue chiton and himation; or you may choose modern dress, with Mars in a modern uniform and with Venus in a blue sundress. It's up to you what you think would fit best with your group.

You will also need participants dressed as Mercury and Iris. Mercury may
wear a Classical white tunic or casual modern clothes. Iris should wear
something rainbow-colored either way.

a white altar cloth

a plate of small cakes or cookies that can be shared by all the participants

The Rite

The altar should be set up with the altar cloth (if you are using one) and the
white candle in the center. The red candle should go to the right and the blue
one to the left. The basket containing the baby should go in the middle of the altar in front of the white candle, with the blanket pulled up so that people entering the room can't see what is in the basket. The libation goblet and bowl should
go before the red candle, and the plate of cakes or cookies should go in front of
the blue one. The incense and holder should go on one end, and the basket for
offerings on the other.

Venus and Mars should not be present or visible. Mercury and Iris will
help people in, show them where to stand or sit, and prepare for the rite.
When all is in readiness, begin with Iris lighting the three candles on the altar.

IRIS: Blessed ones, attend us. We tell an old story today. We tell a story that is
eternal.

MERCURY: [Lights the incense and begins walking *clockwise* around the entire space.] War had come, dark winter. Mars had taken up his long spear,
taken up his brazen helm, put on his armor and his greaves. There was no
joy. There was no brightness.

IRIS: Except his eyes, dangerous and bright. He is the hunter, Red Mars, man
of blood. The sun glinted on his armor, on his upraised sword.

MERCURY: [Returning to the altar and putting the incense down.] His enemies
fell before him, but not all the blood that caked on his limbs was theirs.

IRIS: He too is sorely wounded in body and spirit.

MERCURY: He comes!

Mars: [Enters with a weary gait.] I have returned. But is there anything left? I have won. But will I ever see the moonlight again? Is there nothing but death? I walk in blood, and I shall live until I die.

Venus: [Enters from the opposite side.] War has destroyed the groves. War has ravaged the fields. And yet spring spreads its green haze over the land. The sun glances on the water, ripples spreading where the dragonflies dart. The rain comes down and washes all away.

Mars: [Starts as he sees her.] You.

Venus: You. [They sway, straining toward one another as two lovers who don't yet dare to touch.]

Mars: How can you exist? You are a dream of a time before.

Venus: I am no dream. I am the realest thing in the world. I am joy. I am pleasure. I am hope.

Mars: You are love.

Venus: I am love. [They have slowly approached each other, and now at last embrace.] Love makes us strong.

Mars: Strength grows from love. [They stand in silent embrace.]

Venus: I must show you something! [Pulls him toward the altar, takes up the basket, and folds back the blankets.]

Mars: [Catches breath, bends head.]

Venus: This is Concordia, our daughter.

Mars: It can't be.

Venus: This is Peace, born of War and Love. This is our fragile Peace. This is Concordia, and as she grows she will bring all to fruit. She will restore justice and understanding between people and nations.

Mars: [Goes to his knees.] Concordia. Could such beauty come from me?

VENUS: Could such strength come from me? She is the best of both of us. [They embrace the child together.]

MERCURY: Let us praise Concordia, for after fire comes rain.

IRIS: Let us praise Concordia, for rain brings rainbows.

EVERYONE: Let us praise Concordia.

MERCURY: With her birth, life begins anew.

IRIS: With her birth, the Great Wheel turns again. Winter turns to Spring when her eyes open.

MERCURY: Let us know the blessings of peace. [Pours a libation to Concordia on the altar.]

IRIS: [Takes the plate of cookies or cakes and brings it around the circle of those assembled.] Share in the sweetness of peace. Share in the sweetness of peace.

MARS: We have known much sorrow, and in strife have proved our worth.

VENUS: But now is my season, my love. [Takes his sword and puts it away beneath the altar.] Spring has come. And through it all, our love remains. [Addressing the group.] Simply love.

MERCURY AND IRIS: Turn to one another and greet one another in love.

EVERYONE: [Embraces their neighbors.]

At this point the circle can be broken, and all, including those in the roles of the gods, may embrace one another and the group. Mars should return Concordia to the altar, and those who wish to may approach and leave offerings in the offering basket.

When everyone is done, a shared meal is appropriate. Mercury and Iris should put out the candles and incense and take down the circle.

A Beginning

We have walked through Winter together, and with this rite have come to breaking Spring. What lies ahead in Spring we do not yet know, but we will discover in the course of time what new beginnings it holds for us as the Great Wheel turns and turns again.

Chapter 15

Breaking Spring

As Spring begins, it's time to take a look at the first tasks of the new season. We can expect this phase of Spring to roughly cover the period 2026–2030. Of course all dates may shift depending on actual events, but we can expect the four or five years directly following the resolution of the crisis to be taken up with four tasks: reformation, restoration, healing, and charting a new course. We'll look at each of these in turn, though it is likely that all four will happen concurrently.

Reformation

It is tempting to cast Concordia as the goddess of lawfulness in contrast with Discordia as lawlessness, but that's a considerable oversimplification. Concordia is not simply laws, but rather compacts. Let's look at the difference.

A law is a rule that, justly or unjustly, must be followed, or official consequences will ensue. A law may be good or bad, fair or unfair, appropriately enforced or cruelly rendered. A law is simply a rule that must be followed.

A compact is an agreement. Marriage is a good example of a compact—the parties to a marriage agree on what their vows are, what the parameters of their marriage will be. They decide what is allowed and what isn't, what responsibilities each partner has, and how they intend to relate to one another. Nothing is forced in a compact. It is the free agreement of equals about what the rules will be in their relationship. That is not to say that no partner in a marriage ever regrets their vows or breaks the rules established, as of course this happens, but the compact is freely and openly entered into by people who are able to choose the rules of their relationship. In fact, in US law, a marriage is invalid if both parties do not freely consent. That's why "I do" is the critical part of the ceremony.

The government of the United States has in the past been conceived as a compact. The American's Creed written by William Tyler Page and adopted by the House of Representatives in 1918 begins thus:

> *I believe in the United States of America as a government of the people, by the people, for the people, whose just powers are derived from the consent of the governed.*[66]

In other words, the authority of the law comes from the strength of the compact—the consent of the governed, the people, to submit to the law. It is not derived from divine right or from the acts of the founders, but from the active consent of the people who live here today. We participate in this democracy because the vast majority of us choose to do so, and we have the right to give or withdraw our consent to being governed.

As we reach the last phase of a Crisis era, we look to Concordia to help us create new compacts. We will need them. A crisis alters old rules radically. In order for people to live together in the aftermath, in the nascent new world order, there need to be compacts that set up rules that a majority can agree upon. Three saecula ago, the Crisis era of the American Revolution ended and left us with this question: Now that we are no longer English colonies, what are we? From 1783 to 1789 we debated this fruitfully in state legislatures, newspapers, and a constitutional convention. Our constitution as first written (without later amendments) was the creative expression of the compact that the representatives at the time agreed to. It is indeed a radical work

---

66. William Tyler Page, "The American's Creed," Ushistory.org, https://www.ushistory.org /documents/creed.htm.

for the eighteenth century, encapsulating the ideals of the Enlightenment and the belief that human beings were rational and altruistic actors who would seek the good if given the opportunity. As such, it has been the longest-lasting written constitution in the history of the world.

However, it has changed many times in response to crisis. Will we once again modify it to reflect the needs of a new era? Will we remove the Electoral College, add commitment to the preservation of safe air and water as a right, change the number of states or the way representatives are selected? Will there be other changes that cannot yet be anticipated? It's safe to say that there will be some. The Civil War crisis brought about the end of slavery, a major constitutional change. The end of World War II brought about the "Imperial Presidency," the elevation of the Executive Branch to primacy among the three branches of government. We do not yet know what the end of this Crisis era will portend. We can guess, however, that the rules will change. Hopefully, if we all do our part and this crisis resolves well, Concordia will rule over a new compact, a consensual agreement of what we want to be going forward.

Of course, not everyone will agree. Not everyone will consent. If large numbers of people in certain areas do not consent to the same rules as others, there are two options: force them to comply against their will, thereby breaking the nature of the compact; or allow them to form a different government under rules to which they do consent. For example, let's imagine that 2025 finds three massive splits in the continental United States. California, Washington, and Oregon want a set of rules that closely works with their culture and policies that essentially look across the Pacific to Australia, Japan, Indonesia, and Korea. Texas, Oklahoma, Kansas, Nebraska, Mississippi, Alabama, Arkansas, and perhaps other central states want an entirely different set of rules. Meanwhile, the East Coast has yet a third set of priorities, ones informed by drastic problems of climate change that threaten to make northeastern cities semi-inhabitable as rising seas render them subject to cascading catastrophes. Perhaps there is no single compact to which everyone can consent. Perhaps there is no distribution of resources that is fair. Perhaps there is no single continental cultural model that all these disparate people will consent to adopting.

Can Concordia help us divorce peacefully and respectfully? Can we come to equitable agreements? Or will we attempt to force consent to governance?

We cannot yet know the answer to these questions. We cannot yet know, in full, what the questions will be, though the shape of many of them becomes more apparent each day. In early Spring, these questions will be answered.

Restoration

In the dark of Winter, at the height of the storm, actions need to be taken immediately and with certainty. Many of those actions are temporary measures designed to see us through the moment of crisis. For example, a natural disaster may require the forcible evacuation of an area, as the Fukushima nuclear disaster in Japan did, or the temporary closure of towns and cities that have just been hit. Another example of a temporary measure is rationing. If, for example, we suffer an energy crisis, some form of energy rationing may become necessary. Wars create additional temporary measures—for example, a ban on reporting troop movements while they are occurring. Certain areas may be placed off limits or restrictions may be placed on movement through particular places. There may even be the suspension of normal rules through martial law, curfews, and so on.

In Spring, it's all too easy for temporary measures to become permanent. When can we go back to the place we were evacuated from? When will energy restrictions stop? When will the suspension of normal rules end? One of the major tasks in breaking Spring is to restore the rights and freedoms that had to be put aside during the height of the crisis. Yes, those restrictions may have been necessary, but once the necessity has gone, so should the restrictions.

In the last Spring, we had a lot of trouble with this one, leading to McCarthyism and the excesses of the Un-American Activities Committee. What began as an attempt to prevent Nazi propaganda being spread in the United States in the lead-up to World War II devolved into the infamous "witch hunts" and blacklisting of anyone critical of mainstream views in the mid-1950s. It's easy to get used to temporary measures being the new normal.

One thing we must do in Spring is stop temporary measures that exist to fight threats that are now over.

Healing

You cannot heal from trauma while you are still experiencing it. When you are in the middle of a hurricane, in combat, or refugeeing to a safe place, you cannot be healing from those experiences. Any social worker can tell you that the first thing to do before healing can take place is to get out of the traumatic situation, to be removed from immediate danger. As we move into the late 2020s and the crisis resolves, many people may be able to resume normal lives. Many communities will consider both actual physical rebuilding of destroyed infrastructure and how to incorporate other changes the Crisis era has wrought.

For example, destroyed power grids and power plants may be replaced by modern sustainable power sources and state-of-the-art grids, rather than the coal plants and seventy-year-old infrastructure that was destroyed. New seawalls may protect coastal cities to prevent a recurrence of catastrophic flooding. Physical rebuilding takes time, and much of these five years may be spent on structural reorganization, a process that will create many jobs.

Other changes may be a result of new political borders or the migrations of large numbers of people from one place to another. Just as New Orleans did not recover its former population size and other cities like Houston experienced a considerable influx of people after Hurricane Katrina, so some locations may lose significant population and others gain it. This will forever change the character of both places.

As the land heals, so do the people. Of course many people who have been through these chaotic years have significant trauma to process. However, as lives, borders, and infrastructure stabilize, people will have the chance to heal. For some, it will simply mean resuming their old lives and returning to "normal." However, history shows us that everyone who lives through a Crisis era is changed, even if they were not directly impacted. One of the points of studying earlier Crisis eras, of watching movies like *The Best Years of Our Lives*, is to understand this. In that movie made in 1946, the returning veterans have been changed. However, their families have been too, even if they never experienced bombing or combat. No one can truly return to the people they were before. In early Spring, healing is finding the new normal.

Should the crisis resolve well, for many people the new normal may be better than the old normal. Opportunities arise—education, mobility, social fairness—that were not previously available. New jobs appear to support the new infrastructure. The economic renewal means that more people feel positive about their financial future. Perhaps we will see policies—at least in some portion of the current borders of the United States—that directly impact people in this generation as the GI Bill did in the years after World War II. Student loan forgiveness, universal healthcare, or even a guaranteed minimum income would lift tens of millions of people. A caregiver stipend for those who take care of children, the elderly, or the disabled would help struggling families as the Baby Boomers reach extreme old age. There are many possibilities in early Spring. Some of them will become reality.

Healing rituals for that time are beyond the scope of this book. We do not yet know the course of the crisis, so it is hard to foresee what will be needed. However, healing as individuals and communities will be one of the major things we focus on in the late 2020s. Our invocations of Concordia, both as individuals and as a society, provide a starting place for this process.

Charting a New Course

Sometime around 2030, we will reach Spring Equinox in the great year. We will have begun a new saeculum. In 2030 we will be thinking big. While it is likely that Gen X leaders will hold the most positions of power, they will focus on fixing practical problems with one eye on the mass of Millennial voters who now compose the largest voting bloc. An example of new ideas from the last saeculum was the Interstate Highway System. President Eisenhower, a crusty old Lost Generation leader, envisioned a network of excellent roads that would tie the entire country together—a national road system with standardized signage, standardized lane width, and construction that would allow people to easily drive from one state to another, providing seamless transportation for goods. Sixty-five years later, it is perhaps the most important and enduring piece of national infrastructure. While it's not yet possible to see what it will be, in the early 2030s, look for that kind of project—something that touches every person who lives in the country.

We will likely also be thinking big in our response to climate change. The decade of crisis preceding 2030 is likely to make efforts to respond to climate change small and local. Quite simply, there is no national energy or consensus to do anything more. In 2030 we will get serious. By that point the impacts will be widely felt, and a new era means that new solutions will be apparent. Most importantly, in 2030 the Millennials will range in age from 49 to about 29. They will insist on major responses and their numbers and power will mean that they get what they want. This is one issue that polls as a high concern with a vast majority of Millennials. As they begin to control state legislatures and make their mark in other elected bodies, opposition will become less and less effective.

A New Era

In the early 2030s we will be charting new courses socially, economically, environmentally, and physically. Spring will be fully upon us. The adorable preschoolers will have no memory of the crisis at all. They will grow up with no memory of the Culture War or the constellation of issues that led us to the crisis. In time, in Summer, they will explode into fragments over new issues that are barely on the horizon in 2030. However, that is far away in early Spring, beyond the warm days that are ahead of us.

The world ends and then begins. We will step forward into the new Spring as countless generations have before us. Let us do it with courage and compassion so that we may build things of lasting beauty. The wheel turns.

Bibliography

Aeschylus. *The Oresteia: Agamemnon, The Libation Bearers and The Eumenides.* Translated by Hugh Lloyd-Jones. New York: Bloomsbury, 2014.

Ayton, Mel. *Hunting the President: Threats, Plots and Assassination Attempts— From FDR to Obama.* New York: Regnery History, 2014.

Bedford, Riiko. "Heredity as Ideology: Ideas of the Woman's Christian Temperance Union of the United States and Ontario on Heredity and Social Reform, 1880–1910." *Canada Bulletin of Medical History* 32, no. 1 (Spring 2015): 77–100. https://www.utpjournals.press/doi/pdf/10.3138/cbmh.32.1.77.

Bernstein, Frances. *Classical Living: Reconnecting with the Rituals of Ancient Rome.* San Francisco: Harper San Francisco, 2000.

Bérubé, Allan. *Coming Out under Fire: The History of Gay Men and Women in World War Two.* New York: Macmillan, 1990.

Burton, Neel. "When Homosexuality Stopped Being a Mental Disorder." *Psychology Today*, September 18, 2015. https://www.psychologytoday.com/us/blog/hide-and-seek/201509/when-homosexuality-stopped-being-mental-disorder.

Casey, Michael. "35 Years after Mount St. Helens Eruption, Nature Returns." *CBS News*, May 18, 2015. https://www.cbsnews.com/news/35-years-after-mt-st-helens-eruption-nature-returns/.

Cohen, Adam. "Studs Terkel's Legacy: A Vivid Window on the Great Depression." *New York Times*, November 8, 2008. https://www.nytimes.com/2008/11/08/opinion/08sat4.html.

"'Come Mars, God of War'—The Armilustrium." Wunderkammertales, October 19, 2013. https://wunderkammertales.blogspot.com/2015/01/come-mars-god-of-war-armilustrium.html.

"Constitution and By-Laws of the Martha Washington Salem Union No. 4 Daughters of Temperance." New Jersey Women's History, retrieved April 20, 2019. http://njwomenshistory.org/Period_3/daughters.htm.

Crisafulli, Charlie. "35 Years after Mount St. Helens Eruption, Nature Returns." Interview by Michael Casey. CBS News, May 18, 2015. https://www.cbsnews.com/news/35-years-after-mt-st-helens-eruption-nature-returns/.

Domonoske, Camila. "Why Didn't Officials Order the Evacuation of Houston?" NPR, August 28, 2017. https://www.npr.org/sections/thetwo-way/2017/08/28/546721363/why-didn-t-officials-order-the-evacuation-of-houston.

Euripides. *The Trojan Women and Other Plays*. Translated by James Morwood. Oxford: Oxford University Press, 2000.

"Fact Sheet." Social Security Administration, retrieved December 22, 2018. https://www.ssa.gov/news/press/factsheets/colafacts2018.pdf.

Fejfer, Jane. *Roman Portraits in Context*. Berlin: Walter de Gruyter, 2009.

"Five Borough Food Flow: 2016 New York City Food Distribution and Resiliency Study Results." New York City Economic Development Corporation and the Mayor's Office of Recovery and Resiliency, 2016. https://www1.nyc.gov/assets/foodpolicy/downloads/pdf/2016_food_supply_resiliency_study_results.pdf.

Fowler, W. Warde. *The Religious Experience of the Roman People*. London: Macmillan and Co., 1911.

"Frequently Asked Questions about Pearl Harbor—How Many People Died at Pearl Harbor during the Attack?" Visitpearlharbor.org, retrieved May 18, 2019. https://visitpearlharbor.org/faqs-questions-pearl-harbor/.

Garrett, Phineas, ed. *The Speaker's Garland*. Philadelphia, PA: The Penn Publishing Company, 1905.

Hanson, Glen R., Peter J. Venturelli, and Annette E. Fleckenstein. *Drugs and Society*. New York: Jones and Bartlett, 2017.

Hobbes, Thomas. *Leviathan*. New York: Penguin Classics, 2017.

Homer. *The Iliad*. New York: Penguin Classics, 1998.

———. *The Odyssey*. New York: Penguin Classics, 1999.

Horace. *Carmen Seculare*. Translated by A. S. Kline. London: Poetry in Translation, 2005.

Horowitz, Mitch. *Occult America: The Secret History of How Mysticism Shaped Our Nation*. New York: Bantam Books, 2009.

Horton, Helena. "#RoomForManchester: Kind Strangers Open Up Their Homes to Those Affected by Manchester Arena Attack." *The Telegraph*, May 23, 2017. https://www.telegraph.co.uk/news/2017/05/23/offers-help-pour-social-media-following-manchester-arena-incident/.

Howe, Neil, and William Strauss. *13th Gen: Abort, Retry, Ignore, Fail?* New York: Vintage Press, 1993.

Huber, Michel. *La Population de la France Pendant la Guerre*. Paris: Les Presses Universitaires de France, 1931.

Kerr, Kathleen. "How Did the Reform Agenda of the Minnesota Woman's Christian Temperance Union Change, 1878–1917?" Binghamton, NY: State University of New York at Binghamton, 1998.

"Let's Go to the Movies: The Mechanics of Moving Images." Moah.org, retrieved May 18, 2019. http://www.moah.org/movies/movie_theatres_p.html.

Livy. *Ab Urbe Condita*. Oxford: Oxford Classical Texts, 1974.

Macrobius. *The Saturnalia*. London: Loeb Classical Library, 2011.

Marcus, Sheldon. *Father Coughlin: The Tumultuous Life of the Priest of the Little Flower*. Boston: Little Brown and Company, 1972.

"The Marshall Plan." *Time* 50, no. 4 (July 28, 1947). http://content.time.com/time/magazine/0,9263,7601470728,00.html.

McGee Smith, Charlene E. *Tuskegee Airman: The Biography of Charles E. McGee*. Boston: Branden Publishing Company, 2001.

McManus, Barbara F. "Plancia Magna, Aurelia Paulina, and Regilla: Civic Donors." Vroma.org, retrieved May 16, 2019. http://www.vroma.org/~bmcmanus/women_civicdonors.html.

Mezzofiore, Gianluca. "These People Are Opening Their Homes to Hurricane Florence Evacuees." CNN, September 11, 2018. https://www.cnn.com/2018/09/11/us/evacuees-hurricane-florence-shelter-trnd/index.html.

Miles, Jonathan. *The Dangerous Otto Katz: The Many Lives of a Soviet Spy*. New York: Bloomsbury, 2010.

Morgenthau, Henry, Jr. "Suggested Post-Surrender Program for Germany." Preserved at the Franklin D. Roosevelt Presidential Library and Museum, 1944.

Nash, Tim. "Organized Crime in the 1920's and Prohibition." The Finer Times, November 23, 2008. https://www.thefinertimes.com/organised-crime-in-the-1920s.

"National Depression Glass Association." Ndga.net, retrieved April 20, 2019. http://ndga.net/.

"Nemi Strawberry Festival near Rome." DeliciouslyItaly.com, August 31, 2010. https://www.deliciousitaly.com/lazio-rome-itineraries/nemi-strawberry-festival-near-rome.

Ochmann, Sophie, and Max Roser. "Polio." OurWorldinData.org, November 9, 2017. https://ourworldindata.org/polio.

Ovid. *The Fasti*. New York: Penguin Classics, 2004.

Page, William Tyler. "The American's Creed." Ushistory.org. https://www.ushistory.org/documents/creed.htm.

Place, Robert M. *The Tarot: History, Symbolism, and Divination*. New York: Penguin, 2005.

Regula, deTraci. *The Mysteries of Isis: Her Worship & Magick*. St. Paul, MN: Llewellyn Publications, 1996.

Reif, Jennifer. *Mysteries of Demeter*. York Beach, ME: Samuel Weiser and Associates, 1999.

Ross, Steven J. *Hitler in Los Angeles*. New York: Bloomsbury, 2017.

Russell, Harold. *Victory in My Hands*. New York: Creative Age Press, 1949.

Shakespeare, William. *Julius Caesar*. New York: Simon & Schuster, 2004.

Strauss, William, and Neil Howe. *The Fourth Turning*. New York: Broadway Books, 1997.

———. *Generations: The History of America's Future, 1584 to 2069*. New York: Morrow and Company, 1991.

———. "The New Generation Gap." *The Atlantic Monthly* (December 1992). https://www.theatlantic.com/past/docs/issues/92dec/9212genx.htm.

Summers, Julie. "Children of the Wartime Evacuation." *The Guardian*, March 11, 2011. https://www.theguardian.com/lifeandstyle/2011/mar/12/children-evacuation-london-second-world-war.

Terkel, Studs. *The Good War: An Oral History of World War Two*. New York: Ballantine Books, 1984.

———. *Hard Times: An Oral History of the Great Depression*. New York: Pantheon Press, 1970.

Thucydides. *History of the Peloponnesian War*. New York: Penguin Classics, 1972.

Tilling, Robert I., Lyn Topinka, and Donald A. Swanson. "Eruptions of Mount St. Helens: Past, Present, and Future." United States Geological Survey, 2002. https://pubs.er.usgs.gov/publication/7000010.

Tull, Charles. *Father Coughlin and the New Deal*. New York: Syracuse University Press, 1965.

"25 Avril 1792: Première Utilisation de la Guillotine sur un Condamné." France-pittoresque.com, April 25, 2019. https://www.france-pittoresque.com/spip.php?article5744.

"Viewpoint: 10 Big Myths about World War One Debunked." BBC News, February 25, 2014. https://www.bbc.com/news/magazine-25776836.

"Who We Are." Rhine.org, accessed April 30, 2019. https://bit.ly/2PtGWL7.

Wyler, William. *The Best Years of Our Lives*. MGM, 1946.

To Write to the Author

If you wish to contact the author or would like more information about this book, please write to the author in care of Llewellyn Worldwide Ltd. and we will forward your request. Both the author and the publisher appreciate hearing from you and learning of your enjoyment of this book and how it has helped you. Llewellyn Worldwide Ltd. cannot guarantee that every letter written to the author can be answered, but all will be forwarded. Please write to:

Jo Graham
℅ Llewellyn Worldwide
2143 Wooddale Drive
Woodbury, MN 55125-2989

Please enclose a self-addressed stamped envelope for reply,
or $1.00 to cover costs. If outside the U.S.A., enclose
an international postal reply coupon.

Many of Llewellyn's authors have websites with additional information and resources. For more information, please visit our website at http://www.llewellyn.com.